OMAHA HIGH-LOW

How to Win at the Lower Limits

D1004695

OMAHA HIGH-LOW

How to Win at the Lower Limits

★────────────────────────────★

SHANE SMITH

CARDOZA PUBLISHING

Cardoza Publishing is the foremost gaming publisher in the world, with a library of over 200 up-to-date and easy-to-read books and strategies. These authoritative works are written by the top experts in their fields and with more than 10,000,000 books in print, represent the best-selling and most popular gaming books anywhere.

FIRST EDITION

Copyright © 2008 by Shane Smith
- All Rights Reserved -

Library of Congress Catalog Card No: 2007941283
ISBN: 1-58042-222-5

Visit our web site—www.cardozabooks.com—or write for a full list of books and computer strategies.

CARDOZA PUBLISHING
P.O. Box 1500, Cooper Station, New York, NY 10276
Phone (800) 577-WINS
email: cardozabooks@aol.com
www.cardozabooks.com

TABLE OF CONTENTS

৯ Acknowledgments ৯

Tom McEvoy and T. J. Cloutier, tournament specialists and authors extraordinaire, have been supportive and inspirational influences in my life. They have always encouraged me in my efforts to help low-limit players learn how to play poker as well as they do!

My sincere appreciation to Mason Malmuth for assisting me in editing and improving the 1991 version of this book. My thanks to Lou Kreiger, author of *Hold'em Excellence*, who wrote a favorable review of this book in *Card Player* magazine.

ॐ Dedication ॐ

I dedicate this book to the late Don Vines. With his outgoing personality and contagious sense of humor, Don made each of his friends—whether they were buddies from tennis, poker, or law enforcement—feel that they were his best friend. If they deserved a pat on the back, he stroked them for their success. If they needed a kick in the butt, Don obliged them with a friendly reminder to clean up their act. And when his friends needed help, he was always there. Don was first and foremost the best friend I ever had and I loved him dearly.

Early in his poker career, Don played only limit hold'em and Omaha high-low. He was especially proud of the huge trophy he was awarded for winning the Gold Coast Open championship Omaha high-low tournament in 1994. Even after those humongous amalgamations of red and gold plastic, topped by an Oscar-type figure with armed raised in victory, became obsolete, Don kept the relic prominently displayed in his office as a tribute to his tournament triumph. Later in his poker pilgrimage, he began playing no-limit hold'em, and quickly became a frequent tournament winner. Teaming with renowned poker author Tom McEvoy, Don wrote *How to Win No-Limit Hold'em Tournaments*, which became a hit with novice players.

In 2007 the annual poker tournaments played during the national police and fire games in Las Vegas were named in Don's honor. After years of assisting the organization with the tournaments, he is now remembered every year at "The Don Vines Memorial Nevada Police Athletic Federation Poker Tournaments."

Chapter 1

Introduction

If you're new to the game of Omaha high-low, also called Omaha high-low 8-or-better, you're in for a treat. The competition in the low-limit games is usually weak, learning the correct strategies is surprisingly simple, and if you apply the principles presented in this book, you'll find yourself enjoying win after win at the felt.

Omaha high-low is rapidly becoming the game of choice for increasing numbers of poker players for several reasons: there is a lot of betting, meaning the pots are generally full of chips; there are usually multiple winners in each pot; and best of all, a good solid player can really make money at this game. In short, if you want a game filled with action, then Omaha high-low is the game for you.

If you ask average players in a typical game, "How do you win at Omaha high-low?" they will have a range of flawed replies on the hands you should play. Joe may answer, "I only play four low cards goin' in and one of em's gotta be an ace." But Slick won't agree: "I don't fool around with no low-card hands 'cause I don't like gettin' split up. So just play big high hands and you'll come out okay." Then Doreen contradicts Slick with, "I want a chance at both ends of the pot, so I only play hands with both possibilities—two high cards and two low cards, suited of course." And Spud refutes that with, "But then you've gotta be makin' two draws and sweating that out. You're better off with three low cards and a high kicker."

If you try to apply all this confusing advice and play by the seat of your pants, you'll have a few laughs, win some pots, lose a lot of them with second-nut lows, and fade away into the Omaha sunset with a bunch of losses.

The real answer to "How do you win at Omaha high-low?" is actually not that tough. I'm going to show you how to make money against the Joes, Slicks, Doreens and Spuds out there by giving you a set of practical and proven guidelines.

My goal is to give you the winning tools to make money at low-limit Omaha high-low poker games and to entertain you along the way.

Until one is committed, there is hesitancy, the chance to draw back, always ineffectiveness. Concerning all acts of initiative and creation, there is one elementary truth: The moment one definitely commits oneself, then Providence moves too. A whole stream of events issues from the decision, raising in one's favor all manner of unforeseen incidents and meetings and material assistance, which no man could have dreamed would have come his way.

—W. H. Murray

Once you decide to play Omaha high-low better than anybody else, and begin to channel all your efforts toward that goal, people and circumstances will bend over backwards to help you become a success.

— The Poker Doctor

Chapter 2

Omaha High-Low: Pluses & Minuses

Every poker game has its own built-in edge. Omaha high-low has several for both the expert and the aspiring player.

ON THE PLUS SIDE
High Action

Omaha high-low is a haven for players who love action. The pots are frequently multiway, raised and big. The chips in the middle of the table can rise as high as the Andes, and calls are more frequent than AT&T's busiest hour.

Live Players Love It

Cappelletti (*Cappelletti On Omaha*) describes high Omaha as a game in which the fishermen (experts) are pitted against the fish (novices, loose players and other undisciplined sorts). The glitter of all that gold seems to be ample bait to suck them into Omaha high-low pots like quicksand gulps down the unwary. However, most loose players either learn to tighten up or they go belly up, a circumstance that is true of any poker game.

Players With Average Skills Can Be Successful at Omaha High-Low

This is not to say that a mediocre player can be a whopping success at this or any other game. However, an average player enjoys a wider margin for success than he does in limit or no-limit hold'em because so many low-limit Omaha high-low players actually play the game very poorly. Also, players do not need to use as many of the stratagems common to other poker games. Therefore, a player's general poker knowledge need not be as extensive. This is because the most useful and most common play in Omaha high-low is the simple, straightforward bet with a playable hand.

An expert poker player accustomed to playing at the higher limits may suffer from his decreased ability to put his opponents on an *exact* hand in loose low-limit games where it is not unusual for six or more players to enter the pot. A friend of mine who plays high-stakes pot-limit Omaha recently played a low-limit Omaha high-low tournament in Las Vegas and bombed out very early. "They were so bad I couldn't beat them!" he lamented. Of course the real expert inevitably shines in any poker game.

Not Many Players are Experts at Omaha High-Low

Omaha high-low is a comparatively new game, although it has become increasingly popular in the cardrooms in California, the walk-in casinos in Las Vegas, and Internet cardrooms around the world. Still, the pool of expert players is shallow. With a modicum of experience, general poker savvy, and close observation of what does and doesn't work, a player can enter this arena armed with about as much potential for success as anyone else.

However, as it peaks in popularity, success will require more and more expertise. I am seeing far fewer juicy games today than there were in 1989 when I first began playing. Players now have access to excellent books on Omaha high-low as well as DVD training programs with game simulations. In short, the opposition is wising up. Giving you the winning edge against your opponents and entertaining you along the way is the goal of this book.

ON THE MINUS SIDE

This fascinating, high-action, mega-pot Mecca for low-limit players has its drawbacks too. You'll meet the grumblers who bemoan its addictive qualities. And the less-skilled players who play too many pots and then complain about its volatility as their stacks yo-yo up and down from hand to hand. Plus, the card squeezers—those converted lowball players accustomed to slyly squeezing their cards slightly apart when they look at their hands—who cry about how frustrating it is to get counterfeited on the river. Here is a list of several characteristics of Omaha high-low poker that some players believe are detriments to their enjoyment of the game.

Decreased Ability to Use All the Ploys of Poker

One dyed-in-the-wool hold'em player described it this way: "I can't disguise my hand; I can't check-raise the turkeys to get 'em out; I can't bluff the pot; I can't even slowplay for profit. What's left?!"

What's left is the straight-out bet, the occasional disguise, the rare check-raise with the opposite-nut hand, the now-and-then slowplay, and the almost-never bluff. Omaha high-low is a *bet 'em when you get 'em* game.

Although it's tough to know where you are 100 percent of the time, the expert Omaha high-low player who plays nutsmanship is still a favorite to win in the long run, even though he may not be able to use his entire bag of poker ploys all the time.

The Pot Usually is Split

Because the two ends of the rainbow meet on the river in Omaha high-low, each will probably win only half the pot. (Note my frequent use of such definitive words as "probably, usually, sometimes, almost" in describing this game. That's the nature of the beast!) Therefore, when a player calculates his percentages in Omaha high-low, he must consider whether he is going for the entire pot, one-half the pot, or (ugh!) one-quarter of it.

It is not unusual for the nut low to be quartered. That is, the high hand wins one-half of the pot, and the two low hands win one-fourth each. In these cases, a low player will lose money (unless there are four or more players in the pot), although winning his share of the pot. "If I win one more pot, I'll go broke!" lamented an old-timer.

Equally frustrating, yet more rare, is the single low hand taking one-half the pot, while two equal high hands split the remaining half. And the most dastardly disaster of all—one high and three lows, each low hand receiving one-sixth of the pot!

Because of the multiway-split potential of many pots, it becomes very important to put players on hands as early as possible. What often causes you to be quartered is that your opponent will make a backdoor hand (a flush, for example), giving him one-half the low plus *all* the high portion of the pot, leaving you with a measly quarter. Of course, in many cases, your adversary had the nut low along with you, but he also had a *redraw*. Redraws give you the possibility of making either a better hand than you presently have, or a second hand in addition to the primary one you are drawing to. A redraw is an important weapon that fells many an enemy.

Low Hands Often Prevail Over High Hands

Low hands are very powerful in Omaha high-low. When there is the possibility of a split pot (when three low cards are on the board), a superior low hand can capture the entire pot by making a low straight or a wheel (A-2-3-4-5), whereas the best high hand usually has only a split-pot possibility. For this reason, some Omaha high-low aficionados will not enter a pot without a powerful low-hand draw.

When they see two low cards fall on the flop, high-hand players moan because they know they're facing a probable split-pot future. One-way high hands that have no low draw lose much of their value when the flop comes with two cards lower than a 9.

At the same time, you'll see a twinkle in the eyes of low-card players, who perceive the advent of a *hogger* for their draw-to-the-wheel hands. Though it is not a melodious word, hogger aptly describes the happy snorts and contented grunts of a happy player who makes a wheel on the river and wins the entire pot. No more beautiful word exists in Omaha high-low poker, unless it be the two-syllable lyric tones of "Nut-Nut!" That's music to the ears of an Omaha high-low player, provided he himself is singing it!

The River is Where it's at in Omaha High-Low

Timidity, reluctance to go the distance, fear of negative consequences—these attributes have no place in Omaha high-low. More hands are either made or destroyed by the profitable or devastating currents on the Omaha high-low river than in hold'em. Because of the nine-card hand each player holds, the power of the final board card in promoting or demoting any hand sometimes seems limitless.

One player told me that he will not go to the river without twenty outs! Another needs sixteen, another only eight. Wherever your style of play lands on this numerical continuum, you must be *willing* to see the river to survive in Omaha high-low. Your willingness needs to be tempered, of course, by whether you believe it will be profitable to see the final card, by the odds the pot is offering, and by how much it will cost you to make the trip. This nerve-wracking characteristic of Omaha-high low is, according to one of my poker buddies, what hooks him into the game. He loves the tension and the suspense.

You Must Wait for a Playable Hand

Tight players consistently win at Omaha high-low; loose players do not. In few poker games is a lack of discipline more expensive. But what is a *playable* hand? Most players agree that the most playable hands are those in which all four cards work together in some fashion. But the tendency of many impatient players is to play hands that are "three-legged," meaning that one card doesn't fit with the other three. And some converts from hold'em often play "two hold'em hands," such as J-10-5-4, thinking they have two straight draws, one high and one low.

Eventually, these loose players become intoxicated with the action and bored with the waiting (a disastrous combination) and begin throwing in chips on every round faster than Jordan used to score points. One such crony said to me, "I don't know what a good hand looks like anymore, so I just play them all." This philosophy is *not* recommended for Omaha high-low. It is the ultimate bankroll buster.

Fluctuations in Fortune

If you play optimum strategy, you should find that your bankroll fluctuations in Omaha high-low are the lowest of any other poker game. Based on my observations of top players, this certainly is true. However, in most Omaha high-low games that I have played at the lower limits, this is simply false. Why? Because so many players enter pots with hands that have a low win expectancy. In other words, they play bad poker!

Therefore, if you choose to play this game for its mega action, its excitement, and its profit potential to high-risk draw hands, you will need a bankroll that is bottomless. In fact, mathematician Mason Malmuth believes that you will go broke fast, no matter how big your bankroll. At the very least, your stack will yo-yo dramatically.

In Omaha high-low, you must consider both the nut low and the nut high hand. You want a low hand *with a redraw*. If you do not hold both ends of the winning potential, your win will be one-half (or one-quarter) of the pot instead of the whole enchilada. This further decreases your win-rate expectancy. With less control over the outcome of your betting strategies and with each player having a four-card hand with (optimally) six duets of cards to which he can draw, you are probably nuts if you are not drawing to the nuts in low-limit games.

CONCLUSIONS

Every poker game has its upside and its downside. Minimizing the perils of loose play and impatience—and maximizing the skills of starting with only premium hands— will help you advance rapidly. Once you've learned to read other players' hands fairly accurately, you'll quickly become an expert player who wins way more money than he loses. This book is designed to help you achieve that financial goal!

Chapter 3

Personality Profiles

Many players who are whizzes at hold'em are washouts at Omaha high-low. They simply do not have the personality traits necessary to become a top Omaha high-low player. Accustomed to the faster paced hold'em, they become bored with the snailish Omaha high-low. Or, having been rammers and jammers in hold'em, they try the same tactics at Omaha high-low, underestimating the impact of the river and burning out in a blaze of frustration.

Former lowball players fare much better. They seem to have acquired the patience it takes to wait for playable hands and the endurance required to take big draws. Seven-card stud people sometimes have trouble in reading the common cards, forgetting that duplication can kill a hand (although, not necessarily), and that they can play only two of their hole cards.

So who are the players who become the leaders of the pack in Omaha high-low? They are people who possess most of the following characteristics.

PERSONALITY TRAITS OF SUCCESSFUL OMAHA HIGH-LOW PLAYERS
Patience
If you are impatient and easily tire of the waiting game, try something else. Omaha high-low is not your bag.

Even Temperament
Steam easily? Go on tilt when you get drawn out on? Tend to tear off the door hinges when your 20-out hand bites the dust on the river? Do not, at risk to your remaining mental stability, play Omaha high-low.

Nerves of Steel
If you have the unflappable nerves of a brain surgeon, you've found your ideal operating room in Omaha high-low. Any physician worth his stethoscope is a good diagnostician, knowing when (and when not) to take his patient to the table. He also has endurance enough to stay with the scalpel until the surgery is finished and does not waver under pressure. If this is you, you're in your milieu in the world of Omaha high-low.

Perseverance
Peace Pilgrim was a middle-aged woman who set out on foot with no personal belongings and no money to walk the

highways of the United States to verify her belief that world peace is achievable in our time. She spent close to 30 years delivering her message of peace and inspiring others to go for it. If you have this kind of *heart*, go for it yourself in Omaha high-low.

Reverence for the River

Remember the rock song, *Rollin' On The River*? If you're willing to sink or swim on the river and if you deeply revere its power, you are ready to take the plunge into Omaha high-low. If not, obey the signs and "Don't Swim Here."

Double Vision

Closely akin to reading between the lines, this skill is requisite to Omaha high-low success. You must be able to determine both the low and the high potential of your hand in relation to the flop. If you don't have double vision, don't head for an optometrist or an Omaha high-low game.

Tracing Ability

Picture a scout in the Old West leading the posse to the secret camp of the bad guys. What does he do? Everything he can to find out where the dudes are hiding. If you can use his skills in tracing the betting so that you can put a player on a probable hand, you are way ahead of the posse. But if you're accustomed to allowing your mind to wander off in the beauty of the Dakota territory, sunset will fall quickly on your Omaha high-low game.

Money Moxie

I don't like to discuss money management because my ideas differ from the poker gurus who tell you not to quit when you're winning and not to quit when you're losing if the game is good. Omaha high-low can have wide swings in fortune for loose players, and there are many of them at the lower limits. It is not unusual for neophytes to lose count and suddenly find themselves tapped out or into the game for several bills. And there is the matter of streaks—the losing kind, the winning kind, and the yellow kind.

So I have to leave this one up to you, but as for me, I like to quit when I have either won enough to satiate my basic avaricious nature, or when I have lost so much that either my bankroll is in jeopardy or I am no longer perceived as being a competitor. I don't have a rich uncle to call during a disastrous losing streak, but if you do—and if you play too loosely—call him now rather than later. You'll need his deep pockets before you get in too deep.

PERSONALITY TYPES WHO PLAY OMAHA HIGH-LOW

Omaha high-low attracts a melange (that's French for "weird mixture") of player personalities. The sooner you can typecast characters playing on your stage, the faster your profits will build. Although the following descriptions are written in generalities and with a touch of humor, I think you'll find an underlying grain of truth in each one.

Lowball Larry

Larry's a refugee from cardrooms that used to spread only lowball. When the faster-action hold'em games became legal, he felt like a displaced person. Then he found a game he could identify with in Omaha high-low. Larry discovered that if he waited (patience is his forte) for only those hands with A-2-3-X suited, he could win most of the time. Bingo!

Larry's not lost anymore. But *Wise Wanda* (we'll meet this character later) watches him closely, and she's learned that when Larry is in the pot, she'd better bow out with less than the nut low.

Reckless Rick

Last week, Rick made a killing at the track: His long shot came in at 16-1! Today, he has his bundle with him and just knows that his long-shot (synonymous with *losing*) hands are going to come in too. And that's why Rick raises randomly, ready to sink or swim on every pot he plunges into. You will sink with him, carried away by the tides of intemperance, if you fall into his maelstrom. Rick's cousin, Loose Louie, and his uncle, Action Al, will also be pushing your head under the waters if you don't haul out your life preserver.

Passive Paula

Paula's prime ploy is the check-call. She's not ready for the perils of betting, probably because she is playing with scared money. But she will call with the nuts (raising is risky), check her ace-high flush (you can't be too careful), and (this may be a Ripley's item) bet her wheel *if* she's sure that no one else has one.

Tight Ted

Ted wears a watch with a timer and alarm function, plus the usual day-date-calendar and stopwatch features, illuminated dial, deep-sea diving capacity, and built-in calculator. About once every 45 minutes, Ted enters a hand. When he hears the sound of the buzzer that he has preset on his watch, he takes a break. When he falls behind $40 or forges ahead by $50, Ted travels. If you've got the nuts but Ted bets first, just call—you and Ted are tied.

CARDOZA PUBLISHING • SHANE SMITH

Hot Harry

When he read his Zodiac this morning, Harry was happy: "Today all your dreams will come true." What better fantasy than making a killing off Larry, Ted, Rick and Paula at Omaha high- low? And right now, it's all coming true: Harry's on a roll and raking in pot after pot. Will it never end? He's ramming and jamming and joking and toking the dealers big. When his heat wave gets too hot, it may be a good time for you to take a break and go buy that decorator tube of Colgate you've seen advertised. Better to donate $5.00 to your teeth than to have Harry's sink further into you while you feed his lucky streak.

New Nellie

Her friend, Adventurous Irene, suggested that Nellie try something besides pan and pinochle. "Just look at your hand and if you have good low or high cards, bet!" she advised. And Nellie does. In fact, she bets or calls on everything, since who really knows what "good" cards are? Rick's ruses ricochet; Paula's puzzled; Harry's about to commit hara-kiri; and even Ted's temperature is rising as Nellie wins pots with 8-6 for low, two middle pair, and a 9-high flush. Only *Wise Wanda* understands that the money Nellie wins is like a temporary loan—in time, it all returns to the lenders.

Expert Eddie

If you're seated in an Omaha high-low game with Expert Eddie, examine your chips carefully: You may never see them again. Not because he is a thief, but because he's got the expertise to outplay most of his opponents. Eddie is affable and often talks a good game while showing down the double nuts with the premium starting hands he always plays.

Although he has over 10 years of poker experience, Eddie still refers to his poker books to brush up on fundamentals and sometimes borrows his brother's poker software programs for practice. You'll see him pausing to trace the betting before he acts, folding when he thinks he is beaten, and leaving when he has met his goals for that session.

Wise Wanda, of course, likes to play in games with Eddie because she learns a lot by observing his moves and trying them for herself. But Loose Larry, Reckless Rick, Passive Paula and Tight Ted are definitely defeated by Eddie's expertise.

WHO IS WISE WANDA?

Who is this Wise Wanda, anyway? She is the *Wisdom Within* each of us, the small voice that always gives us sound advice. Naturally, she is asexual so you could call her Wise Wendall.

If this seems too metaphysical for your scientific blood, then just think of him ... her ... it ... *they?* ... as your most highly-developed subconscious intelligence—that part of you that intuitively knows the right thing to do. The trick is to do it!

Of course, Wanda-Wendall's wisdom is based on extensive study and examined experience, which is the stuff s/he uses to help you always make the best decision.

Wisdom is the reward you get for a lifetime of listening when you'd have preferred to talk.

—*Doug Larsen*

We must believe in luck. How else can we explain the success of those we don't like?

—*Jean Cocteau*

I make progress by having people around who are smarter than I am—and listening to them. And I assume that everyone is smarter about something than I am.

—*Henry J. Kaiser*

Chapter 4

The Basics: How Omaha High-Low is Played

If you already know how Omaha high-low is played, save yourself some time and skip this chapter. But if you're new to the game, here's a quick how-to that will get you started on the winning track.

Since Omaha high-low is a form of hold'em, it is played according to the same basic procedures as limit hold'em, no-limit hold'em, and even pot-limit hold'em. Because low-limit Omaha high-low is played with prescribed betting limits, it is more similar to limit hold'em than no-limit hold'em. The main difference between Omaha games and limit hold'em games is the number of cards you are dealt. Instead of receiving two hole cards like you do in hold'em, you receive four hole cards in Omaha.

OMAHA

Four Starting Cards

HOLD'EM

Two Starting Cards

Another important difference is that in hold'em, you may use zero, one or two cards from your hand to make your best five-card combination. In Omaha high-low, you must use exactly two of your four hole cards and exactly three of the board cards to make your best hand. Also, hold'em is a high game. The only time the pot is divided between two or more players is when all active players have hands of equal value. In Omaha high-low, the pot is usually split between the best high hand and the best low hand. The only time the best high hand wins the entire pot is when no low hand is possible; that is, three or more of the board cards are higher than 8.

With these major differences in mind, let's review the basics of playing Omaha high-low.

The Blinds

The two players sitting to the left of the **button**, which marks the dealer's position (indicated by a plastic disk that says "button"), are called the **small blind** and **big blind**, respectively. They must post forced bets before the deal. The small blind bet must be equal to one-half the small bet, and the big blind bet must be equal to the small bet. For example, in a $4/$8 game, the small blind posts $2 and the big blind posts $4. These are mandatory bets designed to stimulate action by ensuring that players have money in the pot to compete for before more cards are dealt.

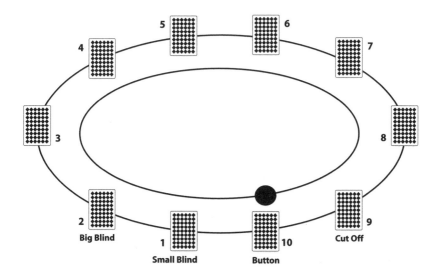

Even in the unlikely event that everybody else folds but you, you figure to have at least the big blind to compete against before the flop. In my experience playing $2/$4, $4/$8 and $5/$10 Omaha high-low, you will have a lot more competition after the first betting round than just the big blind. The number of players who enter pots in low-limit games often ranges from four to seven in nine- or ten-handed games. Sometimes everyone joins the fun before the flop, in which case it's called a **family pot**.

The Starting Cards

As soon as the blind bets are posted, the dealer distributes four cards, called **hole cards**, face down to each player. These hole cards are for you alone to see. They are the cards that you will be using to make your best possible hand when you combine them with the cards that will be dealt face-up in the center of the table. Naturally, no two hands can be exactly alike in both suit and rank, but two hands may be identical in rank alone. For example, you could be dealt

the A♣ K♣ 2♦ 3♦ while someone else could be dealt the
A♠ K♥ 2♣ 3♥.

The First Betting Round (The Preflop)

Play begins with the first player sitting to the immediate
left of the big blind and moves clockwise around the table.
You have four options when it is your turn to act. You can
fold by turning your cards face down and sliding them to the
dealer. This means a player is not willing to match the amount
of the blind bet (and the possibility of future bets above that
amount). When a player folds, he is no longer eligible to
play during this deal and must wait until the current hand
is completed and new cards are distributed to play again.
You can **call** by placing an amount of money equal to the big
blind in front of your hand. You can **raise** by placing exactly
double the amount of the big blind in front of your hand. Or
you can **reraise** if someone has raised before the action gets
to you by matching the previous bets and raises and adding
an amount equal to the size of the original bet.

Bets and raises during this round are in the lower tier
of the two-tier structure. Thus, if it's a $4/$8 game, all bets
must be in $4 increments, and if there is a raise, that too must
be for $4. So, if one player raises the big blind $4 and the
next reraises $4, all players would have to put in $12 to stay
active, or they would have to fold. There is usually a three-
raise limit per betting round, so in the $4/$8 game, the most
that any individual player could put into the pot during the
round would be $16—the $4 blind bet plus three $4 raises.
After the three-raise limit is reached, the betting for that
round is **capped**—no more raises are allowed. However, all
active players would have to meet the full amount of the bets
and raises to continue with the hand.

After everyone has acted and all bets are called, the dealer piles all the bets in the center of the table. These chips, which include the blind bets, are called the **pot**. The pot is the collection of money the players are trying to win.

If two or more players remain, more cards will be dealt. However, if at any point in time just one player remains active, because all his opponents have folded, that player is the default winner and collects all the money in the pot.

The Flop

The dealer now places three cards face up in the center of the table. This is called the **flop**. The player that starts the betting round will be the first active player sitting to the left of the dealer. **Active players** are those players that have not folded and remain to compete for the pot. If both blinds called before the flop, the small blind would act first after the flop. The betting then proceeds around the table in the same manner as it did before the flop, with one exception. Each player has the chance to check by announcing, "**Check**," or by gently rapping the table with his knuckles, denoting that he wants to keep his cards without posting a bet.

Players may check only so long as no bets have been made in the current round. However, once a bet has been placed, all active players must match that bet and any raises that may have been made to stay active in the hand—or they must fold and bow out of competition for the pot. For example, let's say it's a $2/$4 game and the small blind checks on the flop. If the big blind bets $2 and two other players call, the small blind must call the $2 bet also when the action returns to him to stay active or he must fold. Players may no longer check during a betting round once money has been placed into the pot. It's pay or don't stay.

Sometimes, nobody bets on the flop, they all check. In that case, everybody gets to see the next card for free. But that seldom happens in Omaha high-low. A sequence that often occurs is that the first person checks, the second player bets, a couple of other players call, and then the first person either decides to call, raise or fold.

All bets and raises on the flop are still in the lower tier of the two-tier structure. In a $4/$8 game, they would be for $4, and if it was $5/$10 you were playing, they would be in $5 increments.

When the betting is concluded for the round, the dealer will drag all the bets into the pot. If just one player remains, the pot is his. But if two or more active players remain in the hand, you'll see the fourth board card.

The Turn

The dealer will turn over a fourth board card; this is called the **turn**. The betting proceeds as it did on the flop, with active players checking, folding, calling, raising or reraising.

The only exception is that the betting limits rise for this round (and the following one). All bets and raises now jump to the higher tier of the two-tier structure. It now gets more expensive to play through to the end. So if it's a $2/$4 game you're playing, the opening bet will have to be $4 (not $2 as before), and if it's $4/$8, you'll have to put $8 in to make a bet and $8 more (for $16 total) if it's a raise. As in all betting rounds, there is a three-raise limit, so the most that can be bet during this round by any individual player in a $4/$8 game is $32—one $8 bet plus three $8 raises and reraises.

The River and Showdown

When the action on the turn is complete, the dealer again adds the bets to the pot and then turns over the fifth card in the center of the table. This is it, folks—the **river**! This betting round, like the turn before it, is played at the higher tier of the two-tier betting structure.

The river is the ultimate judge of success or failure in Omaha high-low. If you make your hand on the river, you're singing—but if you miss your draw on the river, you're sighing, you're crying, you're losing all those bets! The betting sequence is the same as it was on the turn, except that when the betting is complete, every active player turns over his hole cards so that the dealer can call the winning hands. This is called the **showdown**. He will declare which is the best low hand, which is the best high hand, or which hand has the best of both worlds and wins the whole enchilada—called **scooping**.

THE IMPORTANCE OF THE TWO-PLUS-THREE RULE

The sequence of play for Omaha high-low is simple, just as it is in all forms of hold'em. But many players who are accustomed to playing limit Texas hold'em, in which they can use either zero, one or two of their hole cards to make their best possible hand, have trouble playing Omaha high-low for the first time. Why? Because they often forget that you *must* use two cards from your hand and three cards from the board to make your hand. Exactly two plus three, no variations allowed, is the Omaha rule. The good news is that you can use any two of your hole cards to make your low hand and any two hole cards to make your best high hand, whether they are the same two or a different two, and even if they overlap. And aces can count for either high or low, or both!

Of course, in order for a low hand to be possible, three of the board cards must be an 8 or lower. And you must have two low cards that do not duplicate any of the three board cards to make a low hand. A **wheel** (A-2-3-4-5) is the best possible low hand and, sometimes, it even wins the other half of the pot as the best high hand. When calculating your low hand, neither straights nor flushes count against you. Thus, an ace to 5, all in hearts, is not considered a flush for the low end of the pot (that wouldn't be very low at all!) but simply a wheel—the perfect low! On the high side, however, that ace-to-5 suited hand would be considered a 5-high straight flush, a very powerful hand indeed.

If no one meets the minimum qualifications for a low hand, the player who has the best high hand wins the entire pot. You must turn over *all* four cards to be awarded your share of the pot.

So, remember the two-plus-three rule—two of your hole cards and three from the board.

Chapter 5

Starting Hands Strategy

When you enter the battle for an Omaha high-low pot, it is unwise to go in with any holding that does not adequately outfit you for the upcoming fray. Although fate may dictate the hands you are dealt, its role stops there—you are the one who must decide whether your hole cards are strong enough to enter the battle.

The type of hand you are dealt must fit the cards that the dealer flops. For example, when you are dealt three low cards with a high kicker, and the flop comes with two or more high cards (which do not pair your high card nor give you flush potential), your hand does not fit the flop and you must fold.

Always ask yourself, "What kind of flop am I looking for?" Or establish your flop requirements for each hand you play with an inaudible statement such as, "I need at least two diamonds and a deuce on the flop to continue."

START WITH A FOUR-CARD TEAM

The expert Omaha high-low player looks for a hand in which all four cards work together as a team, similar to the teamwork of a baseball club. If the shortstop misses the ball, the outfielder is there to back him up. But subtract one of the nine starting players and the team cannot compete at its highest level.

Similarly, when you enter the contest with K-Q-J-3, your team of cards is missing an important fourth connector and is handicapped before it ever begins the game. In my experience at the green felt, it seems that the high straight I am drawing to always misses by the one card I am missing when my hand is three-legged.

Ideally, these four cards also contain both a high draw and a low draw. For example, the mighty A♣ K♦ 2♦ 3♣ arms a combatant with multiple layers of armor: two high flush draws, one of which is the nuts; one high straight draw, which would complete a nut straight; the wheel draw, which can capture the entire pot; and even top two pair.

Some Omaha high-low hands have a much higher expectancy for success than others. For example, A-2-3-4 has a far better chance of winning than K-Q-8-8 (which should almost never be played) because it has the potential for winning not only the low, but also the high. Eddie Q, a good low-limit player, will play no hand unless it contains an A-2 suited to another wheel card. He waits a lot, yes, but he also wins consistently at low-limit Omaha high-low poker.

Hands such as A-3-4-Q also have a higher winning potential than a K-K-Q-3 because of their dual high and low possibilities. In fact, seasoned Omaha high-low players will not play the K-K-Q-3 type hands because they are "three-legged"—only three cards work together. Further, the hand has no low-draw potential. In *Championship Omaha*, T.J. Cloutier calls the one card does not work together with the other three cards a "dangler." "It's dangling off the roof someplace," he wrote. And you'll be stranded on the roof without a ladder if you continually play three-legged hands.

The value of Omaha high-low hands is also influenced by table position, because (as in all button games) players who act last have the advantage over players who must act first. Prosperous poker players do not come in up front with weak hands in Texas hold'em, lowball, high Omaha or Omaha high-low, because front position weaklings cannot tolerate bullies who mistreat them by raising, reraising, or capping the pot.

STARTING HANDS GUIDELINE

The following Omaha high-low starting hands guidelines are for players who want to hone their skills in choosing playable hands, thus ensuring that their earnings expectancy is positive. It is based upon my playing experience, the results of a questionnaire answered by seasoned Omaha high-low players, and computer analysis using Mike Caro's *Poker Probe* to test the strength of a particular hand when it is pitted against others.

These guidelines are modeled after the report card system used by teachers. Some hands deserve an A, some get grades of B, others rate a C, and a few tag along with a D. Following the guidelines are a list of Dangerous Draws, troublesome hands that can lead you down blind alleys and into the hands of bankroll bandits.

"A" Omaha High-Low Hands

Play these hands in front position, middle position, late position; in short, play them from anywhere at the table and for any amount. You may enter the pot with a raise, although raising before the flop usually is not done as often as in hold'em. In all flop games, the main reasons to raise are to either build the pot, to knock players out of it, or to isolate your play against a single opponent. Building the pot is the most common reason to raise in Omaha high-low. With very strong hands that have both high and low winning potential, you may wish to keep everyone in before the flop, saving your raise for post-flop action.

Though not a requisite, you would prefer your hand to be suited or double-suited. In Omaha high-low, when we say **suited**, we usually mean that the highest card in our hand is suited to one of the lower cards. Therefore A-K-2-3 suited means that the ace is suited to one of the smaller cards; and A-K-2-3 double-suited means that both the ace and the king are suited to one of the two wheel cards rather than to each other.

1. A-K-2-3 (A-K-2-4, A-K-2-5, A-Q-2-4, A-J-2-3)
2. A-2-3-4 (ace with any three wheel cards)
3. A-A-2-3 (aces with any two wheel cards)
4. A-2-3-x (A-2-3-8, A-2-3-10, etc.)

"B" Omaha High-Low Hands

You may play these hands near the front, in middle position, and in late position. You can call a raise with them, or raise in middle position against weak players, or when there has been little preflop action and you're sitting in a late position.

1. A-2-6-7 (plus A-2 with any pair, A-2-5-10, A-2-6-8, etc.)
2. A-3-5-7 (A-2-J-10, A-3-6-8, A-2-Q-10, etc.)
3. 2-3-4-5 (2-3-4-6, 2-3-5-6, but must flop an ace to continue)
4. A-K-Q-J (A-K-J-10, A-Q-J-10, etc.)
5. A-A-K-K (K-K-Q-Q, K-K-J-J)

"C" Omaha High-Low Hands

Play the following hands in late positions when you can get in cheaply. You may not wish to call more than a single raise. Against strong opposition, pass.

1. K-K-Q-J (and other ace-less four high-card sequences suited, with a pair)
2. K-2-3-4 (king suited with three wheel cards)
3. K-Q-2-3
4. 2-4-5-6 (and other hands with four cards lower than a 7, but without an A-2, A-3, or 2-3)

"D" Omaha High-Low Hands

Play these hands on the button or in the cutoff seat, against weak opponents, or against tight opponents who have given no action in front of you—or when you are feeling reckless and lucky. Remember that "D" also stands for "dog!"

1. A-6-6-8 suited (and similar hands: the lower the odd card, the better)

2. A-K-Q-X (K-Q-J-x, Q-J-10-x, J-10-9-x) These are three-legged dangler hands that might be played in special situations (short-handed play, for example) from late position.

3. Hands such as 8-7-6-5 have proven themselves to be total losers. Even if you make the highest straight possible, you probably will still be splitting the pot with a lower hand. If the flop comes with high cards and you recklessly decide to pit your J-10-9-8-7 straight against any action, you will probably be staring down the barrel of a big gun: the K-Q-J-10-9 nut straight. Another type of hand that is omitted from this chart is 9-9-8-8 and similar holdings with two middle or low pairs.

These starting hands are representative of the types of hole cards to look for in low-limit Omaha high-low. If you like statistics and appreciate the value of knowing the odds of how a particular hand performs against others, I highly recommend that you study *Omaha High-Low: Winning Strategies for all 5,278 Omaha High-Low Hands*, by Bill Boston. With almost 150 pages of statistical charts, the book assigns a rank to every possible Omaha high-low hand. The hand that merits the number-one spot on the charts? A-A-2-3 double-suited. My favorite hand to play, A-2-3-K double-suited, ranks 44th.

Many experienced players will not play any hand that does not contain an A-2 suited with a backup wheel card—or so they tell me. Even they have been known to stray upon occasion!

WHAT IS AN EXCELLENT OMAHA HIGH-LOW STARTING HAND?

It doesn't take a rocket scientist to answer this question. The best Omaha high-low hands are capable of capturing both the high and the low ends of the pot. They also have all four cards working in unison, with redraws to even better hands. And that's why A-K-2-3 and A-A-2-3 are such powerful holdings.

A-K-2-3 (Double Suited)

King Midas would exchange his gold for this starting hand. What makes it so powerful is its nut-nut potential. It makes a nut high straight, a wheel, one nut flush, one second-nut flush, and even top two pair. I've seen players hang onto this hand even when only one low card came on the flop with only one card matching their two suits, and end up winning the nut low or making the flush with two running suited cards. How many flops can you think of that would induce you to fold this hand?

Omaha Starting Hands Chart

"A" Omaha High-Low Hands

Play these hands in front position, middle position, late position; in short, play them from anywhere at the table and for any amount. You may enter the pot with a raise, although raising before the flop usually is not done as often as in hold'em.

1. A-K-2-3 (A-K-2-4, A-K-2-5, A-Q-2-4, A-J-2-3)
2. A-2-3-4 (ace with any three wheel cards)
3. A-A-2-3 (aces with any two wheel cards)
4. A-2-3-x (A-2-3-8, A-2-3-10, etc.)

"B" Omaha High-Low Hands

You may play these hands near the front, in middle position, and in late position. You can call a raise with them, or raise in middle position against weak players, or when there has been little preflop action and you're sitting in a late position.

1. A-2-6-7 (plus A-2 with any pair, A-2-5-10, A-2-6-8, etc.)
2. A-3-5-7 (A-2-J-10, A-3-6-8, A-2-Q-10, etc.)
3. 2-3-4-5 (2-3-4-6, 2-3-5-6, but must flop an ace to continue)
4. A-K-Q-J (A-K-J-10, A-Q-J-10, etc.)
5. A-A-K-K (K-K-Q-Q, K-K-J-J)

"C" Omaha High-Low Hands

Play the following hands in late positions when you can get in cheaply. You may not wish to call more than a single raise. Against strong opposition, pass.

1. K-K-Q-J (and other ace-less four high-card sequences suited, with a pair)
2. K-2-3-4 (King suited with three wheel cards)
3. K-Q-2-3
4. 2-4-5-6 (and other hands with four cards lower than a 7, but without an A-2, A-3, or 2-3)

"D" Omaha High-Low Hands

Play these hands on the button or in the cutoff seat, against weak opponents, or against tight opponents who have given no action in front of you—or when you are feeling reckless and lucky. Remember that "D" also stands for "dog!"

1. A-6-6-8 suited (and similar hands: the lower the odd card, the better)
2. A-K-Q-X (K-Q-J-x, Q-J-10-x, J-10-9-x) These are three-legged dangler hands that might be played in special situations (short-handed play, for example) from late position.

Aces With Two Wheel Cards or Two High Straight Cards

Aces are powerhouses to hold'em players, who often risk mountains of chips raising with them before the flop. They are important in Omaha high-low, too, but are not nearly as powerful as they are in Texas hold'em or high Omaha. However, line them up with two suited wheel cards and you have the potential to make aces full, two nut flushes, and a wheel for a high-low scoop.

When you hold the mega-high hand of aces suited with a K-Q or a K-K, your chances of scooping the pot are excellent—if the flop arrives with no low cards. However, if it comes with even one low card, many inveterate low drawers will hang in to the river for their chance to win half the pot. And if no low cards flop, you usually don't win a very big pot because the low players are not in it trying to outdraw you with a potential nut low. So, because it has only high potential, this hand is not as strong in Omaha high-low as aces with two wheel cards, even though it looks mighty pretty.

A-2-3-4

Four wheel cards with ace-suited. Rocks love this one, especially former lowball players who hide under it like snakes seeking shade. When the flop comes with two or more low cards, they coil, ready to strike on the turn. The power of this hand lies in its potential to make a wheel, which often wins both high and low; the nut flush or the nut low.

Four-Wheeler Without an Ace

Hands such as 2-3-4-5 or 3-4-5-6 are playing hands from late position in Omaha high-low. They can make a wheel when the ace flops, a low straight (which can capture both high and low), and even a straight flush if they're suited (for which you'll sometimes win a nice T-shirt from your cardroom). Because many A-2-only holders are counterfeited when an ace or a deuce flops, this lowly hand moves in on them like a sniper and shoots them down from the treetop.

However, if the ace does not flop, the four-wheeler has a greatly reduced chance of making the nut low. With no ace on the board, the 2-3 holding is a dangerous call for low, because two other lows beat it (A-2 and A-3). Further, when you make only a low straight for high, you almost always must split the pot with the nut low.

Because this hand has so many other options, it is usually a worthy holding, capable of calling a raise before the flop from late position. Just recognize that when there is a lot of raising before the flop, most of the aces are out and your chances of flopping an ace are greatly reduced.

OVERRATED HANDS
A-2 With No Backup Low Card

With no extra outs for a low draw, this hand often gets counterfeited. It seems to be a cruel trick of Lady Luck that the counterfeit card usually arrives at the river, after it has cost you a bundle to draw to it.

A-A Without Connectors or Suited Cards

Pocket aces are far more powerful in hold'em and high Omaha than in Omaha high-low. For example, suppose you have A-A-9-6 and the flop comes A-10-4. Anyone with a hand such as 2-3-4-5, K-Q-J-10, or A-2-3-10 will be drawing to it. If another wheel card appears, you will lose to a wheel; if a high connector flops, you could lose to a high straight.

Usually, you cannot raise players out of big draws in a multiway pot. Keep in mind that low-limit games are almost always played multiway, with four to nine players in every pot.

K-Q-Q-X and J-J-10-X Without Connectors or Suited Cards

Big pairs are also stronger holdings in high Omaha than in Omaha high-low. They work better at the higher limits in Omaha high-low, where the pots are generally contested by fewer players; that is, you have fewer people to outdraw. (Cloutier and McEvoy discuss the important differences between low-limit and high-limit Omaha high-low in *Championship Omaha.*) High hands lose value (especially the three-legged ones) when two low cards appear on the flop. Play them cautiously, if at all.

Four Low to Middle Cards in Sequence

Expert players will usually fold hands such as 3-4-5-6 or 4-5-6-7 before the flop. They know that when a low straight is possible, a nut low usually is also out there. In essence, they have a draw for only half the pot with no potential for a scoop unless the A-2 is on the board. Of course, the lowest end of a high straight usually is also a stone cold loser.

"Boston's Bandits"

What are the three worst cards in Omaha high-low? They are 9, 8, and 7, which are in more losing hands than any other cards. Bill Boston calls them "The Three Bandits." In fact, if you are dealt the 9♥ 8♦ 7♣ 6♠, Boston points out that the rank of your hand is 4,691 on his chart of 5,278 Omaha high-low hands. And the very worst of these three bullies? The

9, "as it is still possible to win with the 8 or 7 in your hand, since either works for an emergency low." Beware Boston's bandits! They're bound to steal your chips.

An Underrated Hand

The double-flush draw, with the potential for a backdoor flush gives this hand a powerful extra out that many players underestimate. The nut flush cannot be duplicated by any other hand, and a backdoor flush often does not need to be the nuts to win the pot.

DANGEROUS DRAWS: TAKE A TOSS, NOT A LOSS

These hands are like some celebrities: On the surface they look good, but beneath the make-up, the water's pretty shallow. Chips march away from stacks in legions during the play of these hands. However, good things sometimes happen to even the bad guys, and occasionally these hands will come in for you.

Top and Bottom Pair on the Flop

All too often someone else holds top pair and second pair to beat you, making this one a vulnerable draw after the flop. But even more fragile is second/third pair, especially if the flop has come with all low cards.

For example, suppose you hold the A♠ 3♠ 5♥ 8♥. The flop comes 3♦ 5♣ 10♣. What are your draws?

a. Another 5 gives you the third-best full house, fives full of threes, when the best hand is tens full and the second-best is fives full of tens;

b. Another three gives you the fourth-best full-house;

c. A deuce on the turn makes a wheel (and a 6-high straight) possible for someone else;

d. Another club makes a flush possible.

This hand is a good example of a preflop beauty turning into a post-flop bag of bones.

A-2 With No Other Outs

Most Omaha high-low players enter the pot with this type of hand, but it is weak and often gets beaten because it has no additional low draw. (Unfortunately, it seems as though the counterfeiting ace or deuce too often comes on the river, when it is the most expensive.) Take a toss, not a loss.

Lowest Set on the Flop

Making the lowest full house in this game can be a costly disaster. If you think someone else has higher trips at any point in the betting, fold this hand. Don't let low trips trip you up.

Third-Nut Flush Draw

The second-nut flush is expensive enough when someone else has the nuts. The third-nut is often financial suicide, unless you backdoor it, that is, the flop comes unsuited, with two running cards in your suit on the turn and river. Better yet, the flop comes with two spades (one of your suits) and a heart, and then shows two running hearts (your other suit).

Second-Highest Straight

If it's possible for a higher straight to be made, someone will usually make it. Murphy's Law always seems to prevail.

Second-Nut Low

With multiple people in the pot, second-nut low usually loses. One reason for this is because many skilled players will check their nut low to the "driver." The driver is the player with the highest possible high hand at any point in the betting, and often controls the pot by betting or raising. The nut-low often checks to the driver either to disguise the strength of his hand, to entice a bet from the second-nut low, or because he has no redraw to a better low in case he gets counterfeited on the turn or river.

CONCLUSIONS

The value of a strong starting hand in Omaha high-low cannot be overestimated. "Omaha high-low is a hand-value driven game," T.J. Cloutier said in *Championship Omaha*. Unlike the stock market, which fluctuates the value of even the best stocks, blue-chip hands never vary in their importance to your winning potential. Unfortunately, these hands are as elusive as the fabled butterfly of love and they are just about as hard to catch.

And that brings up one of the most important character traits of strong Omaha high-low players—patience. Waiting goes against the grain of impatient players, those antsy nail biters, chip fiddlers, compulsive callers and players who seek continual action. After awhile, all hands seem to have potential and they begin entering pots with rags. You'll hear them say, "Who can tell what a good Omaha high-low hand is, anyway?" And you'll see their stacks shrinking like mud in the desert sun.

Some Omaha high-low players carry business-card sized reminders to the green felt, with a list of their starting hands written on it. Others use positive affirmations such as those listed below to remind them not to fall into the Tilt Trap, which often snaps its jaws on your emotions and turns you into a weeping wimp when you take a bad beat.

AFFIRMATIONS

Affirmations are mental reminders that you program into your subconscious. They are always positive, personal and present tense. People in all walks of life use affirmations to remind them of their goals and personal priorities. When you find yourself joining the ranks of the restless, try the 3-W's affirmation: Wait, watch, win.

1. **Wait** for a premium starting hand
2. **Watch** for a flop that fits it
3. **Win** your share of the money

Just one disclaimer to the power of affirmations: They do not take the place of skill and they do not substitute for discipline. They augment skill and discipline with a positive mental attitude that helps keep you off tilt and on target.

In Omaha split, no starting hand has any intrinsic power in and of itself. It must mesh with the flop. Otherwise, fold it as quickly as you would a rag.

—*John Payne*

It is okay to always play your best poker.

—*Mike Caro*

Chapter 6

Playing the Flop

Mental preparation for playing the flop is imperative in Omaha high-low. Along with your decision to enter the pot, you should always ask yourself, "What do I hope to make with this hand?" Also, determine what you are looking for on the flop. Ask, "Which three cards will make my hand on the flop?"

What is the ideal flop for my hand?

Picture your ideal three-card flop. For example, if you are holding the A♠ 3♠ 4♦ K♣, say to yourself, "I am looking for the 2♠ 5♠ on the flop and a high spade on the turn." This is the ideal flop for your hand.

CARDOZA PUBLISHING • SHANE SMITH

Or if you are holding the A♦ K♥ J♦ J♠, your ideal flop is two or three diamonds, a 10 or a queen, a jack with (ideally) no overcards, an ace, or (bingo!) Q♦ J♣ 10♦, giving you a made straight, trips and the nut (even royal) flush draw.

What is the ideal hand for this flop?

A question to ask when deciding how to proceed on the flop is, "What kind of hand would be ideal for this flop? Do I hold it?" And, "Is there a player in this pot who almost always enters pots with the four cards that would best fit this flop? Who is it?"

When the dealer turns the first three cards revealing 77 percent of the cards available (including the four that you hold), you are faced with the most important decision you will make—hold 'em or fold'em. Read 'em and weep or, hopefully, read 'em and reap.

Fit or Fold

The cardinal principle for determining whether to continue with a hand is this: fit or fold. No matter how pretty your hand was going into the flop, if it doesn't fit, you must fold it. For example, when you hold high diamonds and the flop comes with clubs that do not enhance your draw, you must fold. Or if the board shows all low cards and you hold a high hand, fold because the low hands have the potential to make wheels and low straights that can capture the entire pot.

One of the biggest mistakes poker players make is falling in love with a preflop hand and not being able to break their engagement with it. Chronic callers and other loose players lose mega chips by not being able to disengage their emotions from their card sense. They chase in a dogged effort to make their beautiful hands come in. But no matter what you've heard, beauty does *not* lie in the eyes of the beholder: It lies in fitting the flop.

IF IT'S POSSIBLE, IT'S PROBABLE

Another important concept to take into account when you play Omaha high-low is this: If it's possible for someone to have a higher high or a lower low than you do, it is probable that they do.

It is not unusual for the nut-low player to smooth call the betting, an especially deceptive move. He does this for two possible reasons:

1. He may think there is another nut low out and he stands to get quartered;
2. If no one else also has the nut low, he doesn't want to scare out the second-nuts and lose that money from the pot.

For example, with three people in the pot—two of whom hold the nut low, with only one of them holding the high hand—the two low hands will split one-half the pot (each receives a quarter of it), while the high winner will receive all of the other one-half.

Low-limit Omaha high-low is a game of the nuts. If you don't have them or a draw to them, you are in jeopardy—unless, of course, you're pretty sure that no one else does either. This is especially true for low hands, because they can be duplicated in two or even (disaster!) three places at the table.

Many players enter a hand with an A-2 "bare;" that is, without other options. Therefore, calling with the second-nut low is often disastrous. Even an A-2 stands to win only one-quarter of the pot if someone else also holds it. More rare is a nut-high hand, such as the nut straight, being quartered by the nut-low hand, but it happens. In fact, everything incredible happens in low-limit Omaha high-low because the pots are usually multiway, each player holds a nine-card hand, and the river card has the power to drown even the strongest of swimmers unless they have an extra out to use as a life jacket.

Having completed your mental chores, you can greatly enhance your chances of profitably playing the flop by asking the following questions. Correct answers will lead you to a quality decision.

SIX KEY QUESTIONS
1. Does my hand fit the flop?
There are six types of flops in Omaha high-low—low, high, flush, straight, paired and ragged.

    a. Low—two or three cards 8 and below
    b. High—two or three cards 9 and above
    c. Flush—two or three cards of the same suit
    d. Straight—two or three cards in sequence
    e. Paired—two cards of the same rank
    f. Ragged—three unrelated cards

When your hand is a straight holding such as K-Q-J-10 and a paired board flops, you are out of synch with the flop. If your hand includes a high pair such as Q-Q-10-9 and the first three cards on the flop are wheelies (wheel cards), you should abandon ship because high pairs do not usually fare well against a wheel-draw board. Ideally, the flop should be the same type as your hand.

If you hold a low hand and the flop comes with two or three new low cards, you are in excellent position to capture the low end of the pot, especially if you have a good wheel draw (which may win it all). When the flop contains two or three high cards, and you have a high hand that matches them, be ready to play your hand aggressively.

When the flop has two or three unsuited cards that give you eight to 16 outs to make the nut straight, you are in good shape. But beware! It is not unusual for the board to present two running flush cards on fourth and fifth streets, thus voiding the value of your straight. For this reason, some expert players do not play this hand aggressively unless they also have a backup flush draw. But heads up, fire away! Smart opponents will not drive a medium straight until the river. In fact, they will fold it on the flop if they believe that it has a negative expectation of holding up on the river. For example, take a look at this hand and flop.

THE FLOP

YOUR HAND

What's Your Best Move?

Even with his made straight, not only will an expert player not bet it aggressively, he will play it cautiously. Why? Because there are so few safe cards remaining in the deck — another heart may make a flush for someone else, and a 9 can make a jack-high straight for an opponent. You would need two running cards — a king plus a board pair — to make the nut full house (and then hope no one makes quads when the board pairs), or two running spades (including the ace) to make the nut flush.

When you hold cards that will make the nut or second-nut flush, and the flop comes with two or three of your suit, again you are in position to drive. However, be cautious in pushing a second-nut flush. The number of king-high flushes beaten by ace-high flushes seems to be astronomical in Omaha high-low. The check-call may be your best alternative with a second-nut flush when you are in a front position, *if* you choose to continue with it at all.

If the board shows either a high card (preferably the highest rank on board) that matches your pocket pair, or a pair that matches one of the ranks in your hand, again you show potential for a winning result, provided your trips are not the lowest possible.

If the flop shows three unrelated cards, there is often very little action when it hits, so that if you hold any promise for either a low or high draw, you can continue to play. But unless you flop trips, your best strategy is usually to wait and see.

2. If I make my hand, will it be the nuts?

Suppose you hold the Q♦ J♦ 10♠ 9♠ and the flop comes with two low diamonds. Ask yourself, "If I make the flush, how likely is it that I will win the pot?" Less-than-nut flushes, unless you backdoor them, are legendary for biting the dust in Omaha high-low. Just as dangerous as making the third-nut flush is making the second-nut straight because it is often harder to get away from.

If you don't have the potential to make the top straight, even if you flop the temporary nuts, you are in danger. It is not unusual for a straight to be counterfeited in Omaha high-low, especially if you flop it. As demonstrated in the previous hand example, many seasoned players will not bet a straight aggressively until the river unless they have other draws with it. (This goes against the grain of many converted hold'em players who play straights aggressively.)

Another danger point is flopping the middle or low set when there are higher ranks on the flop. Nothing can be more demoralizing than making the second-nut or third-nut full house. In a recent Omaha high-low game, this scenario took place:

FLOP   **TURN**   **RIVER**

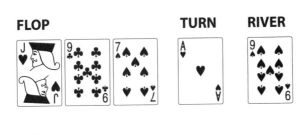

BOB

DICK

LARRY

Bob flopped top set (jacks), Dick flopped bottom set (sevens), and Larry flopped an open-ended straight draw with an overpair of aces. The turn showed an ace, giving Larry top set. When nines paired on the river, Bob thought he had the winning hand and lost a $200 pot with jacks full, the second-nut full house.

Hooked into the betting with his lowest possible full house, Dick left the table moaning about a bad beat. But was it a bad beat or simply bad judgment? Sitting in a late position, he called the preflop action with a weak hand. When Bob bet into him on the flop, he could have thrown in a comparatively inexpensive raise to probe the strength of his opponent's hand. Bob would probably have reraised, at which point Dick could have dropped the hand without further loss.

3. How much of the pot am I drawing for?

Because so many Omaha high-low pots are split, it is imperative that you decide whether it is worth your investment to take the turn. Do you have the potential for winning the whole pot, one-half the pot, or only one-quarter of it?

Players who draw with the nut low when they are fairly sure that there is another nut low out, will lose money at the river unless they are in a multiway pot. Of course, most low-limit hands are played multiway in contrast to high-limit Omaha high-low, which usually has fewer players in pots. Cloutier and McEvoy discuss this and other vital differences between the two games in *Championship Omaha*.

One player aptly remarked, "If I keep winning with my ace-deuces, I'll go broke!" What he meant is that the nut low is frequently held by more than one player, which usually leads to each one of them winning only one-quarter of the pot. It is important to place other players on hands as early as possible, so that you can determine how much of the pot you are drawing for. Few decisions are as important to your winning potential.

If the flop arrives with more than one low card when you are holding a high-only hand, it is likely that you will share the pot with a low hand if you win the high end of it. It is also likely that you will lose the entire pot if the lows make their wheels and you don't have a higher straight or flush.

It is almost impossible to force out the low draws with a high hand (such as trips), when there is more than one low card on the flop. In fact, some premium low-hand holders cannot be raised out even if only one low card comes on the flop, especially if there are five or more players in a raised pot, giving them what they perceive as favorable odds to draw for two running low cards on the turn and river.

You must ask yourself on every flop whether the odds are in favor of your winning the entire pot, or whether you are competing for part of it. In business terms, will the amount of money you must spend to play out the hand give you an adequate R.O.I. (return on investment) to make it worth your while? How aggressively do you want to play?

No matter what the pots odds nor how much money is in the middle, some players allow the remote possibility of winning the pot to take precedence over prudence. This can be a fatal flaw in your poker strategy. As Mike Caro states in *Caro's Secrets Of Poker,* "In the long run, in poker, you don't get paid to win pots—you get paid to make the right decisions."

4. How many players are in the pot?

Some hands play admirably against multiple opponents, while others stand up better against one or two. If there is little money and few players—and if you can probably win only half of it—you should lose interest quickly to save your chips for a more promising situation on a future flop.

However, if you are heads up against another player and if you think that you are both playing high only, you may win the entire pot and thus make it worth your while to take a big draw. But drawing for a straight, for example, in a small pot against two opponents when you stand to win only half the pot is an unprofitable play.

It is when there are few players in the hand, little money, and you are facing a probable split pot that you should bow out early.

5. How much money is in the pot?

The amount of money in the pot is directly proportional to the number of players who have entered it, and/or the amount of raising before the flop. To determine whether to continue, ask yourself, "How much money can I earn in relation to my bet if I win this pot? Half the pot? One-fourth of it?"

Using standard odds tables such as those in Bill Boston's *Omaha High-Low* will give you an idea of your winning expectancy versus your investment. You should also ask yourself, "How much money is likely to be in the pot at the river?" This is the principle of implied odds. Again, ask yourself, "How much of the pot do I stand to win?" Your answer will depend in part upon your ability to put other players on hands. If you can determine who probably holds the nut low and who most likely is coming in with a high draw, you will be better able to decide where you are in relationship to them.

By asking yourself how much money is in the pot, how much will probably be there on the river, and how much of it you can win with your hand, you can make a quality decision. All class players do this automatically.

6. Was the pot raised before the flop?

When players hold a super low hand such as an A-2 suited to one or two wheel cards, they tend to raise before the flop. Some also raise with big high hands (a pair of aces with connectors, for example.) If you hold an A-3 and the flop contains three low cards that do not include an ace or a deuce, you must assume that someone has the A-2 in a raised pot. Therefore, you should ask yourself whether it is correct to continue, hoping that a deuce will appear on the turn or river to counterfeit the A-2 holder and thus make your hand. Also, you have to consider whether the holder of the probable A-2 would be likely to also have the trey, thus giving you only a quarter-pot potential even if you make your hand.

Assuming that you hold a high hand in a raised pot and catch a high flop, you then need to consider whether it is likely that the raiser(s) flopped trips higher than yours, a higher straight draw, or a better flush draw. In other words, should you play the hand cautiously or ram it full steam ahead?

Important knowledge in deciding whether to continue past the flop includes:

a. Knowing the kinds of hands players most frequently raise with;

b. Understanding who usually plays low hands and likes to raise with A-2 suited;

c. Knowing who would raise only with a high hand. How do you learn these things? You *watch* while you're *waiting* so you can *win* more. Those affirmations again!

Because there is more money in raised pots, and because the quality of hands is likely to be higher, you should seldom enter the pot with less than premium cards. And you definitely should not continue past the flop unless you hold either the nut hand or have a draw to it.

CONCLUSIONS

Deciding whether to continue past the flop is one of your most important decisions in low-limit Omaha high-low. Making weak draws based on emotions rather than pot odds, holding onto a hand that was a beauty going in but turned into a beast after the flop—these are costly errors. Instead, base your decisions on sound reasoning.

Wasn't it Ben Franklin who said, "A penny saved is a penny earned?" Do you suppose he played poker?

Chapter 7

Taking the Turn

Rudyard Kipling may not have been a poker player, but he gave sound advice to turn takers and decision makers:

I have six faithful serving men,
They taught me all I knew:
Their names are what and where and when,
And why and how and who.

Omaha high-low players are well advised to take Kipling's quote to heart by asking these six powerful questions on the turn. Your ability to answer them as precisely as possible will guide you in evaluating your hand correctly and deciding how to proceed.

In poker as in life, success hinges on making optimal decisions. In Omaha high-low every turning point demands a reevaluation of your potential for winning the pot. The greater your ability to correctly answer these six questions, the better your chances of making the right move with "the right stuff."

SIX TURN QUESTIONS
1. Who is in the pot?

You must know your competition: their MO's, their likelihood of slowplaying or raising, and their probable holdings. Most games have their share of rocks, loose geese and maniacs, because in Omaha high-low there is "something for everybody," even a reasonable player like you.

Against loose players and maniacs who love the fast action this game offers, there is a less likely chance that they are holding a premium hand than if one or two Tight Teds are in the round. And so, if you have a good draw and a known loose player raises on the turn, you may feel somewhat more comfortable in calling or even reraising to test the waters. However, if Wild Willie *does* have the best hand, prepare yourself for a fast ride on the midnight express because loose, aggressive players will raise and try to cap every betting round. It is often more difficult to play against maniacs than more predictable opponents because of their sometimes unexpected holdings. And when one of their rag hands comes in to beat you out of the pot, it can put you on mega tilt.

In contrast, if you hold the second-nut high or second-nut low draw and a rock raises, you may reasonably assume that he possesses the nut hand. Then you must reevaluate your chances of holding the best cards, especially if three low cards, three flush cards, or a pair is on board.

Ask yourself, "What could he possibly be raising with?" Based on your observations of his style of play and tracing (recalling) his betting on the flop, you then decide your best response. Good advice: If you don't hold one of the nut draws, fold against a tight player's bet or raise.

Another thing to consider on the turn is this: "Who is on the button or in very late position?" Even though you may feel comfortable in calling a loose player's raise with your second-nut full house, if an expert player on the button also calls, take it seriously. A sophisticated player in late position in a tight game is apt to smooth call a bet on the flop with the best hand, deferring his raise to the turn or river when many players feel committed to calling even a double raise in order to protect their investments in the pot. Of course, that is flawed thinking, because once money is in the center, it no longer belongs to you. Blind money is not an investment, it is a dividend in the event that you can cash your "bonds" in a favorable stock market transaction.

2. What could they be holding?

After analyzing the betting patterns of your opponents, ask this question: "What could they possibly be holding?" This is the skill of putting them on a hand, figuring out what your opponents' hidden cards are, becoming a poker Peeking Tom.

Putting players on hands is a question-and-answer thinking process. "What could Tight Ted possibly hold to call on the turn? What cards could have prompted Wild Willie's raise? What must I hold in order to call him? What could Loose Larry be drawing to? What am I drawing to? What card do I need to make my hand? If I make it, what are the chances that it will be the nuts?"

It is quite likely that only the skilled players at the table ask these questions of themselves. Experts intuitively ask them before they act at any betting point. This discipline gives them a distinct advantage over less-skilled opponents who enter the fray like jousters wearing a blindfold in the heat of battle, trying to topple the other rider off his horse.

3. Where are the nut draws?

Imagine this scenario: You are in a five-way pot sitting in third position. Player One comes out betting and Player Two calls. With two people left to act after you, what are your chances of being raised if you also call Player One's bet? If you are raised, is your hand strong enough to call the double bet? (This is a good reason to remember that the earlier your position, the more important it is to come in with premium hands.) Remember, too, that it is more likely for any player to call a raise when he already has one bet in the pot than if he has none. In other words, many players find it easier to call $20 in increments of $10 each than to cold-call a single $20 bet.

If you have answered the question, "Where is the player with the nut draw sitting?" it is far easier to decide whether to raise, call or pass. If you believe the nut draw is yet to act and is likely to raise, you may decide to fold if you hold only a mediocre hand. However, if the nut draw is sitting in front of you—and therefore must act before you do—and if you think that you have a good possibility of drawing out on him or of making the opposite-nut hand, you may call.

You would probably raise only if you wanted to limit the field, rather than build the pot. This is true in Omaha high-low because the players left to act after you are just as apt to fold as they are to call or reraise, depending on their hands. If they fold, you have limited the field of opponents and probably increased your chances of winning on the basis of your current strength, possibly without any help from the river card. If they call or reraise, and you call their action, you may be in for trouble on the river and find yourself drowning in a sea of raises by sandbaggers (slowplay artists) who have the advantage of acting after you do.

Where you sit in relation to other bettors is very important. A player who holds the mortal nuts in a multiway Omaha high-low hand—and who is sitting in last position—has the power of an avalanche over a lone skier. If he holds the nut high and two others hold the nut low, they can only call him. Then he will reap the spoils of an extra person's wager (the additional nut-low player).

If his first raise is on the river, other players may have trouble putting him on a hand, and may make a pot-odds call, hoping he doesn't have what they think he has. "Maybe he's bluffing and doesn't have the nuts. I'd better call just to keep him honest" is one of the self-destructive thought patterns of losing Omaha high-low players. There's no need to play the role of sheriff at a low-limit table. You'll have another hand and another chance to win in about three minutes.

Determining *where* the nut-draw hands are, and deciding whether your position is favorable enough to go against them to the river is a pivotal decision. Generally, you do not call the turn unless you are prepared to also call a raise. Poker is a thinking person's game. Skilled players think first, act later. Amateurs act first, think later.

4. Why am I in this pot?

This is a powerful question to pose at every betting juncture. Essentially, you are asking, "What do I hope to make with this hand?" or "What would be the best possible outcome of this holding?"

If your hand promises to make the nut flush, then you know why you just called a raise on the turn. But if you hold the third-nut flush draw, sometimes called a "slush draw," then why are you in the pot? Usually, it is only with a backdoor flush that a third-nut flush wins the high side of the pot.

Are you in it because you think you have the best made hand? The best draw? The second nut but you think it's good enough to win? A backdoor flush draw? Or a full-house draw good enough to sink the other boats on the river? What hand do you hope to make?

Here's an example to think about. You're holding the J♦ J♠ 9♣ 8♦. The board comes with the 3♣ 4♦ 10♦. What possible hands can you make? You might make the jack-high flush and win the pot. You might make the jack-high flush and lose the pot. The board might pair and you'll lose to a full house, even if you make the flush. Another low card might come out on the turn or the river, in which case you might win half the pot at best. If a player comes out betting on the flop, what should you do? In my opinion, you have only one choice. Fold. A hand that looked nice before the flop looks nasty after the flop.

5. Am I likely to have the best hand on the river?

Nobody intentionally makes the second-best (losing) hand on the river. But because hope springs eternal in the hearts of Omaha high-low players, too many of them take the turn with inferior hands.

Another way to phrase this question is, "Which cards will give me the nuts? Which ones will make my hand the second nuts? What cards will make a hand I don't want?" The point is that you do not want to be drawing dead. Drawing dead means that no card yet to come will make your hand a winner. For example, consider this scenario:

FLOP

TURN CARD

Now look at the players' hands and determine the strength of their draws on the flop and turn.

RICK

JANE

TONY

BOB

Rick's Hand

Rick, a hold'em player new to Omaha high-low, thought, "How can I possibly miss making this hand?" But in fact, he was drawing dead. He had no winning outs. Why? Because no matter what hand he made at the river, he would not have the nuts. If a 10 or an 8 fell, pairing the board, Rick's full house would lose to Jane's higher full house. And if another heart showed up on the river to make Rick's 8-high flush, he would lose to Bob's nut flush. Rick was holding what veterans refer to as "DST," double-suited trash.

Jane's Hand

Jane held a made straight (Q-J-10-9-8) and top set. She had good reason to push with her hand on the flop and on the turn. If the board paired any card on the river, she would win the entire pot. However, if another heart came at the river, she would lose everything to Bob, who would make the nut flush. Further, if a king slid off the deck on the river, she would lose to anyone holding an A-J. And if a jack came on the river, she would lose to anyone holding an A-K. Of course, she didn't know that those cards were not out in any of her opponents' hands.

Tony's Hand

Tony had the same two pairs as Rick on the flop. On the turn he picked up the second-nut low draw. He could not have much confidence in his hand on the turn. Why? Because if he went to the river with it, he could only make the second-nut low if another low card came, unless that low card was a 3. Further, if the board paired with either tens or eights, he would make either the second-nut full house or the third-nut full house.

Bob's Hand

Bob held the nut flush draw on the flop. He made a pair of deuces on the turn, plus the third-nut low draw. Going to the river, then, Bob had a very strong drawing hand. His best river card would be the 9♥. Why? Because it would make a low impossible, it would not pair the board and give anyone a full house, and he would scoop the pot with the nut flush.

A similar situation occurred in a recent low-limit tournament. Sitting in the big blind with K-J-7-6 in an unraised pot, I checked the flop when it came K-J-7 unsuited. Player 3 bet and both Player 6 and I called. The turn showed a jack. I checked my jacks full of kings. Player 3 bet, Player 6 folded, and I smooth called Player 3, an amateur with a short stack who had only enough chips to make one more bet. After an uneventful river card, I noticed Player 3 with chips in hand, ready to throw in the rest of his fortune. I checked, he bet the last of his chips, I called and won the pot. Player 3 was holding A-J-7-4 and had made jacks full of sevens.

It is almost suicidal to play the two lowest pairs on the flop. Top two pair is far superior, and top and bottom pair is at least playable, but those two middle pairs are killers. Player 3 was drawing dead with them and ended up chipless and chairless in Las Vegas.

Again, ask these two questions at every point of the betting: "What is the best possible flop for my hand? What is the best possible hand for this flop?" If you have pinpointed someone other than yourself as being the most likely player to hold that optimal hand, your best alternative may be to fold rather than to make a further investment in a pot for which you could be drawing dead.

Some skillful players will not invest past the turn if their hands have only half-pot potential. For example, if there are two low cards and two high cards showing on the turn with few players in the hand, a tight player with a low draw will fold rather than draw. Of course, if he has an uncounterfeitable low draw against little action and there is enough money in the pot to justify his draw, he will go for it.

If you think your hand will be the winner on the river, play the turn aggressively if that seems to be your best strategy after answering these questions. If you don't think your best possible hand has adequate odds of capturing the pot, abandon ship on the turn so that you won't go down with it on the river. Generally, it is the high hand that bets aggressively on the turn; occasionally, the nut low will push it in a late position, suggesting that he holds the high hand and adding a deceptive ploy to his style of play.

6. How much will it cost me to take the turn? Will the river return be worth the turn investment?

This is the process of analyzing your hand on the flop and then asking "What are my odds of making a hand, and what's it worth if I do?" Take a look at this hand:

FLOP   **TURN**

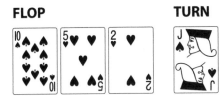

YOUR HAND

Suppose you are in a $5/$10 game, the pot is already $60, and this is a $10 round. An opponent bets in front of you, and a second player raises. Should you call the raise, reraise, or fold? To make a quality decision, you must place a value on each of your outs. A 3 at the river will give you the nut low, a wheel, which could scoop the pot. A queen at the river will give you the nut high. You probably will scoop the pot unless another player also holds an A-K, in which case you'll split the pot. A 6, 7 or 8 will give you the second nut low. A king will make a set for you, but the possible nut straight for someone else. A spade will give you the second-nut flush, which may be good enough to win since you will have backdoored your flush.

After adding up all your outs (cards that will make your hand), assessing the pot odds, evaluating the strength/weakness of your opponents, and calculating what it probably will cost you to go to the river, what is your best move?

MORE POINTERS ON PLAYING THE TURN

The Number of People in the Pot Influences Your Play

The greater the number of people in the hand, the greater the likelihood of your being drawn out on. For example, if you are holding the nut-high hand with two low cards on the board, the turn offers you an opportunity to make it expensive for low hands to draw. When you are fortunate enough to have another player bet into you, you can raise, forcing all low draws behind you to call a double bet (which is four times the size of the flop bet) in order to see one more, very expensive, card.

Conversely, when you have a low draw on the turn and must call a raise to see the river card, you need to seriously evaluate your chances of:

a. Making the nut low;
b. Making a wheel that could scoop the pot; and
c. Getting pot odds commensurate to the risk that you are taking.

Taking your chances with only an A-2 and no other low card is often fatal, for if either an ace or a deuce falls on the river, you probably cannot call the final bet. I highly recommend that you have an extra out for low when you make such a call; for example, an A-2-3-x or A-2-4-Q. All premium low hands possess three wheel cards, including the A-2.

The Value of Extra Outs

The more outs you have at every stage of the betting, the better off you are. For example, in the play of a hand in a $2/$4 Omaha high-low game, John held A♠ 4♠ 4♦ 5♣ in an early position. The flop came 2♠ 3♠ 3♥. When he bet his nut low and nut flush draws, three players called. The turn added the 6♣, giving him the nut low and a 6-high straight with the straight-flush draw. On the river came the 6♠, giving him the nut flush and the nut low, although there was the possibility that someone also had made a full house or quads.

FLOP   **TURN**   **RIVER**

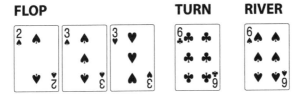

JOHN

All three players called the turn and two called the river, none of whom had either a full house or the nut low. John's extra outs (the flush draw and a third low card) won the entire pot for him. (I have no mathematical foundation for this observation, but it seems that more often than not, when the board shows two pair, no one will have a full house and usually a flush, straight or the high trips will win the high end of the hand.)

Playing the Nut Low on the Turn

Generally speaking, tight players will not raise with the nut low on the turn because they are afraid that someone else may also hold it, leading to a quarter-pot financial return. However, if the wheel is possible, most players will raise with it because of its whole-pot potential, regardless of whether they believe someone else may also hold a wheel.

If an expert player thinks that someone else may still be drawing to the wheel (when he already has one), he will raise to discourage anyone drawing out on him. If you are the player drawing to a wheel when someone else probably has already made one, why draw to it yourself?

Another reason the expert may raise is because, if someone else also makes a wheel on the river, he stands to win only half the pot. And if there is a higher straight possible—for example, the 6-high or 7-high straight if 3-4-5 is on the board—he will win only one-fourth the pot if he has to share his wheel with someone else.

Loose players, however, will raise their wheels indiscriminately, disregarding the probability that another person also holds it or that a higher straight is out. When this happens, the loose player often suffers recriminations such as dirty looks and derogatory comments from the original bettor.

Playing the Uncounterfeitable Nut Low

If you hold an uncounterfeitable nut-low hand on the turn, you may bet or raise with it. **Uncounterfeitable** means that no card yet to come can invalidate your holding, even if it duplicates one of your hole cards. I suggest raising under these circumstances:

1. You think that you hold the only nut-low hand;
2. You are fairly certain that several loose players will call your raise, thus building the pot;
3. You think that you may be able to confuse the high draws enough so that, if you make your hand on the river (even though it may not be a wheel which could scoop the pot), they too may drop their hands. This works especially well if you are a known tight player.

Here is an example of a nut-low hand capturing the entire pot: In first position, Ron held the A-2-J-10 unsuited. The flop came 3♠ 8♠ Q♦. Ron bet and three players called. On the turn came the 9♠, making a flush possible. Again Ron bet with his made straight and the nut-low draw. Players B and C called, but D folded his queen-high flush, thinking that Ron (a known tight player) held a higher flush. When the 7♥ fell on the river, Ron made the nut low and the nut straight. When he bet, both B and C called with second-nut lows.

FLOP   **TURN**   **RIVER**

RON

Ron scooped the pot, leaving D moaning about folding his flush. This semibluff paid off big for Ron, who recognized the value of deception and who had that extra out which so often makes an Omaha high-low hand.

CONCLUSIONS

If you have a made nut-high hand on the turn, usually play it aggressively. If you have an uncounterfeitable nut low, bet, but use discretion in raising, because you do not want to flush out callers who may add to your profit at the river. And you definitely do not want to be quartered if another bettor also holds the nut low.

If you have neither the nut low nor the nut high, but have a premium draw, call if the pot odds warrant it. Or raise if you are an aggressive player and have an exceptionally strong draw. For example, you hold the A♠ 2♠, there are two spades and two high cards on the board, and you are in late position with the possibility of scooping the pot if a spade comes on the end.

And after having done all the right things, beseech Lady Luck to float you a river card that will not sink your ship.

♣ ODDS OF MAKING AN 8-OR-BETTER LOW

You Hold:	Odds of Making 8-or-Better Low
4 Different Low Cards	
Before the flop	49%
2 new low cards in flop	70%
1 new low card in flop	24%
3 Different Low Cards	
Before the flop	40%
2 new low cards in flop	72%
1 new low card in flop	26%
2 Different Low Cards	
Before the flop	24%
2 new low cards in flop	59%
1 new low card in flop	16%

In the lower limits ... there are two kinds of games. The first is when people are playing too loosely. The second is where the players pretty much know what they are doing. In the first kind, after the flop, draw only to the nuts. In the second kind, play correctly and tightly on the flop. Play fewer hands than most before the flop.

—*Ray Zee*

Chapter 8

Rollin' on the River

The Omaha high-low river has currents that challenge the ferocity of the Amazon. Its waters may be hotter than Old Faithful or colder than Lake Tahoe, as choppy as the cool Pacific or as placid as the warm Atlantic at sunrise. Rumor has it that more fortunes are made or lost at the river in Omaha high-low than on Wall Street. Although that is an obvious exaggeration, there is no doubt that in few other forms of hold'em is the river card as important as it is in Omaha high-low. As one player aptly announced to his Texas hold'em buddies, "Omaha high-low's a river game, not a flop game."

Even the expert player who has exercised optimal strategic maneuvers will occasionally find himself ready to tear the deck into shreds as his nut low gets counterfeited on fifth street or his nut flush is drawn out on by some prude from Pasadena holding Q-8-3-2 and making deuces full of treys on the river.

One evening, a player in my hometown cardroom did exactly that. "How much does a deck cost the house?" he asked. After tossing its price to the dealer, he shredded every card in his hand and piled it like New Year's Eve confetti into his ashtray, stopping very short of setting it afire with his vintage Zippo.

River rats courageous enough to raft down the Colorado through the Grand Canyon hire an experienced guide to navigate for them. Here are some tips that will help you steer your way through the rapids of the Omaha river, starting with pointers for playing the nut-high and nut-low hands.

NUT-HIGH AND NUT-LOW HANDS
Playing the Nut High

When you hold the nut high hand on fifth street in Omaha high-low, you live in the best of both worlds: You are in position to capture at least half the pot if there are also low callers in the hand and you win the whole enchilada if no low hand is possible. For this reason, you bet, raise and reraise as much as you can, particularly if you are pretty sure that no one else also holds the nut high. Recall that it is not unusual for high straights to be duplicated in someone else's hand.

Optimally, you have three or four others vying for the pot (as is usually the case in low-limit games), and so the more you can bet, the more you will probably win. Play aggressively with the nut high hand. And hope that what happened to Hapless Harry twice in one session doesn't happen to you: His nut full houses were beaten on the river by quads and a straight flush!

Playing the Nut Low

As much as you want to believe that you have the only nut low, you should be fairly certain about it in order to be aggressive with it, even on the river. If someone else also holds the nut low, you will win only one-quarter of the pot. In the event that only three of you are in the pot, you will lose money to the high hand. If there are four or more players (with two nut lows and one nut high), you still only break even or make a few dollars at best.

If you are in last position and think that no one else also has a nut low, raise. If you are in a front position with several bettors left to act after you, either bet your hand or check-call, rather than check-raise. Although this may seem contrary to your natural tendency to always raise with the best hand, it is often the correct strategy because:

a. There may be another nut low to act after you, in which case your raise will force him to call (or even reraise if he thinks that you hold the high hand). But you will lose one-fourth of your bet to the single high-hand player if you and another nut low get quartered by the high hand.

b. A second-nut-low hand who has not put you on the nut low will be more likely to bet or call if you check, thus increasing the size of the pot—a profitable deceptive play sometimes used by sophisticated players.

WHEN TO PLAY THE NUT LOW AGGRESSIVELY

If you are first to act—sitting in front of the player who has been driving the high hand—and if you are certain that he will bet, you may check your nut low. Then, after the high hand makes his wager and (hopefully) the players who must act after him have called, you can raise. But check and raise only if you are certain that no one else holds the nut low. The check-raise is not as profitable in Omaha high-low as it is in other poker games. Use it sparingly.

Ordinarily, I do not recommend slowplaying anything in Omaha high-low, but I do suggest conservative play with the nut-low hand in almost all situations and positions. However, there are some notable exceptions to this general rule. Here are four situations when you may opt to play the low hand aggressively:

a. When your nut low is a wheel and no higher hand is possible;

b. When the game is loose and you think several loose players will call you with the second-nut low;

c. When three players are in the pot and you believe the other two are both betting high hands;

d. When you are first to act and may be able to disguise your hand by betting first, which sometimes leads the high draws to believe that you are betting the nut high. This scenario happens most often when you have been the first bettor in the other rounds and a scare card such as a flush card or one that pairs the board arrives on the river. Occasionally, the high hand will pass and you may win the whole pot with your low and only a pair (your extra out) for high.

PLAYING THE WHEEL

When your nut-low hand is the wheel with no better hand possible on the board, be aggressive with your betting, even if you know that someone else also has a wheel: The two of you will split the pot anyway. But if a 6-high or 7-high straight is possible and you believe that another player has made it, play conservatively if you also believe that you and the third player both have the wheel and will get quartered by the higher straight.

Take a look at the following scenario, which illustrates a fairly common situation with low hands:

FLOP   **TURN**   **RIVER**

YOU

HAL

DORA

a. Both you and Dora have wheels, but Dora also has a 6-high straight.

b. Hal holds both a wheel and the nut 7-high straight.

c. With $300 in the pot, Hal will win one-half of it for the high straight ($150), and another one-third of the low half of the pot ($50) for a total of two-thirds of the pot.

d. You and Dora will each receive only one-sixth of the total pot ($50 each), giving you a minus return on your investment.

Even in pots where there are only two of you, each of whom has made a wheel, if the 5-4-3 are among the common cards, your opponent will win three-quarters of the pot if he holds a hand such as A-K-6-2 and you have only the A-2. Consider these kinds of possibilities in playing your wheel hands.

For instance, if you are fairly certain (based on the betting) that your opponent has a wheel, you may wish to check your hand to him if you are first to bet. If you are second to act and a player has bet a "wheel" board in front of you, it often is wise to simply smooth call if you do not possess 2-6 or 6-7.

If you bet first and your opponent raises, usually do not reraise with anything less than the A-2-6. Call only, for he is likely to hold the A-2-6 (or A-2-6-7), in which case you will win only one-quarter of the pot if you have the wheel.

SECOND NUT-HIGH AND NUT-LOW HANDS
Second-Nut High

Whether you call with the second-nut high at the river depends upon the betting. If there have been no raises and the driver checks, you may feel safe in wagering on your second-nut high hand. But if the driver continues his thrust, you are in danger of losing your bet if you call. However, there are some circumstances when you can bet or call with the second-nut high:

a. The board suddenly changes character on fifth street. For example, two running suited cards appear on the turn and river making a flush possible. You believe that the former driver has been betting a straight and you have made a medium-high flush. If he again bets, call only; but if he checks, take the initiative and bet.

b. The driver is a known bluffer and you believe that your hand is at least equal to his. Remember that successful bluffs are rare in Omaha high-low.

c. The driver is sitting in last position and either a threatening or a disappointing card appears on the river. A threat may be a third suited card or a board pair; a disappointment could be no third flush or straight card. If you suspect that he was on a draw that is different from what the board shows at the river, you may call his bet with a reasonable hand. If he had been drawing on the come to a busted flush, your two pair may be the best high hand.

Now, suppose you have been the aggressor pushing with your nut straight. The board either pairs or a third flush card drops at the river. Be prepared to sink in its muddy waters if an entirely new bettor initiates the wagering. He probably has made his flush or full house and your nut straight is no longer any good. Remember that if it's possible, it's probable. Why else would the new bettor have stayed in the hand against an opponent who obviously had a made straight on the flop or turn? Fold. Fold fast.

Players who have difficulty releasing a hand that probably has been beaten on the river lose unnecessary chips by calling too often. For example, a player whose ace-high flush has just been counterfeited by a paired board. But because it is not unusual to have a straight drowned at the river by a flush, players usually have an easier time in folding them.

In a ring game at the Orleans Casino's $4/$8 daily game in Las Vegas, a rock player sitting to my right entered the pot in first position. Sitting with A♣ A♦ 6♣ 7♦, I called his opening bet and was followed by three other callers for a total of seven people in the pot including the two blinds. I later regretted not only my decision, but the entire day as well!

The flop came 5♣ 9♣ 5♦. The two blinds checked, Rock bet, and having fallen in love with my suited aces, I called as did Player Three. On the turn came the 5♥. Rock checked and I checked fearing that Player Three had the case 5 or that Rock was slowplaying it. Player Three also checked. The river rolled in a genuine piece of seaweed, the case 5♠.

FLOP　　　　　**TURN**　　**RIVER**

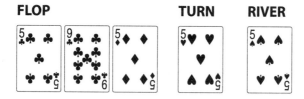

SHANE

Now comes the gruesome conclusion to this tale. Rock bet and I raised with fives full of aces. Player Three folded. Rock reraised and so did I. He answered my challenge by capping it. I called saying something stupid like, "You and I must both have pocket aces." But we didn't: He had pocket nines (pocket nines! A *real* dog hand!) making his nines full of fives a winner over my dog hand, fives full of aces.

As I mucked my cards without showing them, Player Three rubbed some salt into my wounds with, "Boy, I'm sure glad I didn't get sucked in with my pocket aces!" (He probably had read the earlier version of this book, which advises against falling in love with pocket aces, drawing against a paired board, and stumping your toes on rocks.)

Making the second-nut full house at the river is a peril that is sometimes difficult to avoid. For instance, suppose you have been playing your jacks full of eights aggressively. Then a new bettor comes out swinging when a queen washes up at the river. You may safely assume that you have been beaten by either queens full of eights, or jacks full of queens.

The most disappointing full house counterfeit jobs at the river seem to happen to the low full-house hands, those ignorant souls who have been pushing their threes full of deuces or fives full of fours. Then the almighty ace (or some innocuous overcard, such as a 6) falls on the river and an upstart bets out, causing a sinking feeling in the heart of the low full house holder. Use extreme caution in calling when this happens. And of course, always be sure that when you are drawing to a full house, it is the nut full-house draw.

If you hold the nut full house, consider a check-raise only if you are fairly certain that the preflop bettor (who sits to your left) will fearlessly bet his inferior second-nut full house or nut flush. Former nut full house bettors will often feel forced to call your check-raise. But use your check-raises sparingly.

In most circumstances, I recommend the straight-out bet when you make the high hand at the river, and certainly when the texture of the board makes a low hand possible. Betting gives other players the option of calling, passing, or raising—and you don't run the risk of no one betting. Some players show very sheepish faces when they show down the mortal nuts, which they have never bet.

Word of wisdom: Do not wait for someone else to bet your hand for you in Omaha high-low. Usually, if you've got it, bet it.

Second-Nut Low

More hands have probably lost end bets on this hand than in almost any other holding in low-limit Omaha high-low. I hate the second-nut low more than any other thing I can think of in high-low poker. Especially annoying is Tight Ted who has checked his nut low from the flop onward, leaving aggression to the high hands and deceiving you into believing that no one has the low nuts.

If you have good reason to believe that someone has the nut low at the river, fold your hand even if it was the best low until the final moment of truth. If a new bettor, who is not the one who has been driving with the probable high hand, bets when a deuce falls on the river, fold your A-2-4-10 because you probably are beaten by A-2-3-X. This is especially true if the new bettor is someone like Lowball Larry, who usually plays nothing but A-2 with two backup cards to the wheel.

But there's good news, too. If no one appears to have a good low, yours probably is the best one available and you stand to win half the pot with it. This sometimes happens when the ubiquitous deuce falls on the river and the suspected nut-low holder suddenly checks. Now your A-4 is looking very strong and you may bet it, provided no one that you suspect of having a low bets into you, and the only bettor is the person you've put on the nut high. In tracing the betting, if it appears that no one has ever pretended to have the nut low, and if you have the second nut, you can probably feel safe in betting or calling with it on the river.

When Nobody Seems to Have Anything

If there is an optimal time to bluff in low-limit Omaha high-low, it is on the river when an unpaired, non-straight, no-flush-possible board appears. (Of course, these pots are often small because of the minimal action.) If you are holding two high pair or even a pair of pocket aces with nothing else, now is your hour of power. Incredible as it may seem, there are occasions in Omaha high-low when no one has a low hand, even though there are three low cards on board, and when nobody makes a strong high hand either.

The two positions in which you may most profitably advertise a good hand in such a ragged situation are first-to-act and last-to-act. If you are first, it sometimes confuses other players when you bet on the river. "What could he have?" they wonder. "I don't have anything good enough to call with." When you are last to act, they may all suspect that you are bluffing, but since everyone has checked to you, the pot is probably not large enough to contest. Also, no one really knows whether you are betting high or low, so if they have nothing outstanding on either end of the spectrum, they will probably fold rather than waste a bet on a small pot.

CONCLUSIONS

Your profit and loss statement will definitely be more profitable if you play the river skillfully. If you feel glued to the pot at the river and call with what you intuitively know is a loser—Wise Wendall warned you that you were beaten, but you didn't listen to him—you not only go against Caro's advice and Wendall's wisdom, you also lose money unnecessarily. In the long run, you will win more money by "losing" pots that you did *not* call with second-best hands at the Omaha high-low river.

The river giveth and the river taketh away. Make certain that to you it giveth by not giving unnecessary calls to those who taketh.

Uncorrected errors will multiply. Someone once asked me if there wasn't benefit in overlooking one small flaw. "What is a small flaw?" I asked him.

—*Don Shula*

If you know you call too much, you should call less, but not everyone can have complete control over himself. Only the very best do, and even they don't at all times.

—*Ray Zee*

Winning and losing, even when you are on top of your game, usually come in bunches. Limit your losses. Sometimes, it's just not your night!

—*John Payne*

I love one-on-one sports. If anything goes wrong, it's your fault, nobody else's.

—*Hershel Walker*

Chapter 9

Strategic Concepts

This chapter is a collection of miscellaneous winning concepts, general strategies, and other advice to help you maximize your profits at low-limit Omaha high-low by analyzing and refining your game plan.

THE KEY CARD

Each pot you play in Omaha high low will have a key card that you need to complete the hand. Identify your key card before the flop and focus on receiving it.

For example, if your cards are A-2-4-5, your key card for a wheel is a 3. When you have K♠ Q♠ your key card is the A♠ (to be certain that you have the nut flush draw). Every straight requires a 5 or a 10. If one of them is not in your hand, you must flop it to make your straight.

By setting key card requirements for your hand, you can determine whether you will continue past the flop. If you're playing a 2-3-4-6, you will need a usable ace on the flop. You may say to yourself "If an ace does not hit on the flop with at least one other low card, I will fold my hand." (You should be talking more to yourself than to other players, all the time you're playing poker.) Or you might decide, "If the ace doesn't fall on the flop, I'll continue only as far as the turn and only if it's cheap." Note that if there has been considerable preflop action, the aces probably are in the hands of your opponents, since most players who raise have an A-2 with at least one other low card, or a high or multiway hand headed by an ace (or aces) such as A-A-K-3 or A-K-Q-10.

Setting limits in advance on how far you'll go for your key card, depending on the betting, can help you stem a chasing spree.

EXTRA OUTS

Extra outs give your hand a second breath when it is down for the count. Omaha high-low hands have six two-card pairings—each pairing you have adds one more winning possibility to your holding. In *Pro Poker Playbook*, John Vorhaus calls them "packets," an appropriate way to look at an Omaha hand.

In a low-limit ring game, Carl held A♣ K♥ 7♥ J♠ in the big blind in an unraised pot. Two high hearts and one low heart came on the flop. Since Carl was first to act, he was uncertain whether his king-high flush was the nuts. He bet it and had two callers, neither of whom raised. At the river, Carl found out: Ray held the ace-high flush and raised with it. Carl called when the third player dropped out. Why did he call? Because two running low cards had come on fourth and fifth streets, making Carl's extra out, the A-7, good for low and half the pot.

Strong extra outs include:

a.   Double-suited cards;

b.   A low draw with a high card paired to the board;

c.   Straight draws with two cards suited to one of the cards on the board (for a possible backdoor flush);

d.   A low draw with a top-end straight possibility (such as an A-2-6-7 with a board of J-5-4), plus any low, straight or flush draw with an overpair to the board.

In *Championship Omaha,* Cloutier lists many "Tips from the Top." Here is one of them: "Always try to have an extra out." Since he won a bracelet playing Omaha high-low at the World Series of Poker, I'll take his word for it.

DOUBLE-SUITED CARDS

The value of flushes is generally underrated in Omaha high-low. Full houses, straights and wheels can all be duplicated by another player and cause you to either split or quarter the pot, but the nut flush is *the* nut flush. It cannot be duplicated. You have two extra outs to backdoor flush draws with a double-suited hand when the flop shows three cards of separate suits and two of the suits are the same as your two. Most experienced Omaha high-low players will advise you that they would rather make either a straight or flush on the river than on the flop. Why? Because a made straight on the flop often seems to get counterfeited by a higher straight, a flush or a full house on the river, whereas a medium-strength backdoor flush will often hold up on fifth street. Also, many veterans will not play an unsuited hand, unless it contains A-2 with one extra wheel card. You would always prefer your hand to be at least single-suited.

If yours is the type of hand that can counterfeit someone else on the river, it is all the more powerful. Double-suited cards give you such potential, even when one of the suits is only medium-strength, because backdoor flushes do not always need to be the nuts. You don't necessarily need to make the highest possible backdoor flush at the river, just the best one.

THREE-LEGGED HANDS

A three-legged hand is one in which only three of your four cards work together. Playing three-legged hands is a very tempting proposition in Omaha high-low, especially if you hold three cards to a high straight (K-Q-J-6, for example). But for some reason known only to Lady Luck, these hands have cost me more money than my calculator can compute, because it seems that the one card I am missing also turns out to be missing from the flop, turn and river. Unless you are in a very late position in an unraised pot, don't play them. In fact, Cloutier and McEvoy suggest not playing hands with "danglers" under any conditions unless you are in the big blind in an unraised pot.

Also put this hand on your three-legged cripple list: K-K-Q-2, a big pair with one connector and one odd card, especially unsuited. Hold'em players love kings, but expert low-limit players will not play high pairs unless they have two additional options, such as a suited king and a third card to the straight.

One of the few three-leggers you may consider playing is three cards to the nut low such as A-2-3-9. The advantage of these hands over those discussed above is their whole-pot potential if they make the wheel, and their half-pot expectancy when they make the nut low.

SLOWPLAY IN OMAHA HIGH-LOW

Slowplaying almost anything in low-limit Omaha high-low is a mistake. This is not a game in which deception is a prime ploy—save that for your Texas hold'em game. The straightforward bet is usually the best strategy even when you have the nut hand.

Why? Because so many players fish along at the low limits, many of whom don't believe that you have the nuts. Sometimes they are drawing to a higher hand than they've already made; often, that hand is the one you already hold. In other words, they are drawing for a tie. They may think that you're bluffing or they may be loose players (or simply weak players) with second or even third-nut hands. When you don't bet, they get a free card and a chance to outdraw you.

Here is a painful example of not betting when you should. During one of my beginning sessions in a $4/$8 game, I flopped quad threes in the big blind—two threes were on the board and I held two in my hand. I checked and the four remaining players did, too. On the turn came the 10♠. Again I checked, but Marie bet. When the other three players folded, I simply smooth called her, anticipating that I would check-raise on the river. But when the 10♦ came on fifth street and I bet, Marie raised. Her quad tens beat my quad treys.

"Nobody bet on the flop," she explained, "and then I made tens full of threes on the turn." I have not slowplayed low hidden quads since then. However, high quads sometimes can be slowplayed profitably when you have a pair in your hand and a pair comes on the flop. Your hope is that someone will "catch up," make a flush or straight or full house so that you can pound them at the river.

An exception to the rule is, "Do slowplay if you have quads when three of your rank are on the board." This suck-in play may be the only way that you have to make money with a strong hand. When you check your quads, players who hold a high pocket pair will sometimes bet if you check on the flop or the turn.

If the board flops something like 9-9-7 and you hold J-10-9-8, bet on the flop. Players who hold overpairs or a pair of sevens will often call you. The sevens may even raise, which gives you an indication of where you are. Now, suppose a third 9 comes on the turn. You check to create some confusion. The other players will be put to the test of figuring out what you were betting. Sometimes one brave (foolish?) soul will bet—he either has an overpair or he hopes to bluff you out of the pot by representing quad nines.

On the river, you must bet your quads straight out because your call of Brave Soul's bet on the turn has alerted him to the possibility that you have the case 9 and he may not repeat his bet, although chances are somewhat good that he will call you.

Don't slowplay a wheel on the flop, no matter what your position. When three wheel cards come on the flop, at least one or two other players will usually have a wheel draw. Betting your made wheel will force them to call in order to draw for a tie. However, if a fourth wheel card comes on the turn, your prospects of scooping the pot have become dismal. Further, someone may also have made a wheel, plus perhaps the higher straight (6-5-4-3-2).

PLAYING THE STRAIGHT

Even if they have flopped a straight, some cautious players will not bet it until the river. They certainly will not bet their nut straights if two flush cards come with it on the flop, but aggressive players will bet and raise a flopped straight in an attempt to force the low draws, speculators and trips out of the pot.

I admit that I am a Tight Ted when it comes to betting a low straight on the flop. If I don't have an extra out such as the flush draw or a higher straight draw, I don't bet it until the river when I know that it has held up. The bags of bucks I've busted along with my busted straights have taught me this lesson.

Be cautious if you do not hold the key card for the higher straight, and usually do not bet or call if that card comes on the turn or river. For example, suppose the flop comes J-10-8. You hold the nut straight with a Q-9 in your hand. You bet your high straight and have three callers, including Loose Larry. On the turn comes a 7. You bet again and they all call. Guess what appears on the river? The ace. Larry comes out swinging. Does he have a K-Q, which makes the higher straight, or did he pick up a low draw on the turn and has just made his hand? Fold! In either case, you can now win half the pot at best, and why try to do even that with your second-nut straight?

This is a common scenario in low-limit games, where players sometimes chase the pot beyond what seems to be reason. Some of them take the turn trying to make a flush, and then decide to also take the river because with so many people in the hand, their pot odds appear to justify all of their calls. And sometimes, they're right.

THE PROBE BET

Rather than trying to guess whether your hand is the nuts, you can run a "probe" bet from an early position. This bet is similar to the semibluff in hold'em. For example, you make a king-high flush on the flop with only one low card showing. You might bet, hoping that if someone has the ace-high flush, he will raise and you can fold without further loss.

If there are callers but no one raises, check your second-high flush on the turn. Then, if one of the former callers bets, you can decide whether to call him, based on your analysis of his probable holding. If he's a tight player, you may assume your hand is beaten. And then you can do something that's very difficult for most players—fold.

In a recent low-limit game, Player A bet his flush on the flop. Player B, who held the third-nut flush, raised. When Player A reraised, Player B folded his hand. In this play, Player B saved himself the cost of the higher turn and river bets by using a probe raise when it was least expensive.

CHECK-RAISING THE NUTS

When you believe that you have too many friends in your hometown cardroom poker circle, you can shrink it by check-raising, a bet that just about everybody despises. In Omaha high-low, the check raise is used far less often than in hold'em. Generally speaking, I don't recommend it because in the long run, you'll probably lose more money than you make with this strategy.

When you check-raise, you should reasonably expect that someone who must act after you will bet. If you are in a front position and there has been heavy wagering by suspected low hands that you think will continue to drive their lows, you may wish to check-raise on the turn when you make the nut high hand. But if you are in a game in which the nut lows are conservative and leave the driving to the high hand, you probably cannot afford this otherwise pot-building check-raise.

Sometimes, however, even the most deftly executed ploys backfire like worn out mufflers. Holding pocket aces (which seem to be double trouble for me), I once decided to check-raise when the flop came A-8-8, giving me the nut full house. Knowing that any one of the remaining four players was likely to bet a low draw or trip eights, I thought that the check-raise would both limit the field and add to my half-pot winnings in the event that another low card came at the river.

Sure enough, a player bet and I raised. All four of the remaining players called. When a 9 came on the turn, again I bet and they all called. But the unpredictable eraser of fate wiped out my hopes when a third 8 appeared at the river. I checked, John bet and I just called. He triumphantly turned over the case 8 that he had squirreled away along with his nut-low draw 2-3-4-8 hand.

Such is the power of the Omaha high-low river, which once again had washed away the super-nuts like driftwood in a storm. John's call of the check-raise on the flop is another example of the power of the extra out: He had the nut-low draw in a multiway pot and, in the event that it didn't come in, he had that wicked 8.

THE SQUEEZE PLAY

Nothing hurts more than an ingrown toenail or being caught in a squeeze play. It is the Bermuda Triangle of Omaha high-low. First, the triangle: You are in middle position between two heavy bettors who are raising at every opportunity, squeezing your life's blood (your chips) out of you. If you don't hold the nut high (preferably) or the nut low, bow out early, reminding yourself that another hand will be dealt in about two minutes.

Even if you do hold one or the other nut hand, the chances are that one of your two competitors has a duplicate of your holding. In this event, you stand to win only one quarter of a dismal three-way pot. In other words, you will lose 25 percent of your bets by "winning" 50 percent of one half of the pot. Of course, if you think that the other two players hold the opposite-nut hand, you're in high cotton (as Uncle Eugene used to say down on the farm) because you will quarter them and win half the pot for yourself.

Secondly, the squeeze play with a mediocre hand: You sit in second position with two players to act after you. Player A bets on what you believe is the high hand (recall that high hands usually initiate the betting in Omaha high-low). With your second or third-nut low potential, you raise in an attempt to squeeze out other mediocre-draw low hands and capture half the pot.

Or perhaps you are on the button. Player A again initiates the betting and the two other players just call. Now you raise with your mediocre low holding, predicting that Player A will reraise his high hand. Since you have advertised the nut low, Players C and D will be hard-pressed to call the double bet if Player A reraises unless, of course, they indeed have the nut low.

You may also receive a free card on the turn if Player A decides to change his strategy and become conservative. Or if he checks on the turn and your hand is looking better than you anticipated, you might bet hoping that he will raise and force Players B and C to cold-call a double bet. In either case,

you have made a squeeze play which you hope will pay off
for you on the river.

CONCLUSIONS

The more strategies you pack into your lifeboat, the more
likely you are to make a safe crossing of the Omaha high-low
river. Like life preservers, strategy and skill can save you from
muddy waters and rescue your chips from drowning. But one
precaution—don't try to be too fancy in low-limit Omaha
high-low. The overall best strategy is still the straightforward
bet.

Chapter 10

Tournament Tips

Omaha high-low tournaments can be a lot of fun and an additional source of income for expert players. Further, tournaments can teach you how to better play the game. By making a small investment in a low-limit tournament, you can learn some valuable lessons from more experienced players. Also, some people enter tournaments while they're learning a new game in order to limit their financial exposure. That is, you can spend $20 or $40 on a small tournament and avoid risking a $100 buy-in to a ring game.

There are differences in strategy, however, between winning at ring games and winning at tournaments. Players who adjust their cash-game strategy to their advantage in tournaments can increase their win rates significantly.

The following tournament strategies are based on my experiences as a winning Omaha high-low tournament player, discussions with other winners (and losers), and extensive research of the poker literature. I especially recommend *Championship Omaha* by T.J. Cloutier and Tom McEvoy. I owe much of the credit for my success in tournaments to their expert advice.

TIP 1: DECIDE IN ADVANCE WHETHER TO REBUY

The first consideration in designing your tournament strategy is the type of tournament you are playing—rebuy or no rebuy. Since most low-limit tournaments are rebuy events, the techniques discussed here are recommended for tournaments in which you can rebuy (usually when you have less than the initial buy-in amount left in your stack), and add on at the end of the rebuy period.

If you plan to win a tournament that allows rebuys and an optional add-on, enter it with enough money to make two or three rebuys. In most cases, you will need to take advantage of the rebuy option to be one of the top finishers. Therefore, if you are on a limited bankroll, it may be better to save your funds for ring play or for a freeze-out tourney. Your insufficient bankroll will be a significant drawback in playing optimal tournament strategy. Further, if you have entered a small tournament solely for the learning experience, I suggest that you limit yourself to one rebuy at most.

When you go broke, it is usually correct to rebuy so long as you don't overdo it. If you think you're one of the strongest players in the event and there will be a big payoff, rebuy so long as you use discretion in the number of rebuys you make.

Make your decision about adding on at the end of the rebuy period by the size of your stack. If you are very low on chips, it is almost always correct to add on. If you are the tournament leader, it probably isn't necessary to add on. And if you are in a middle chip position, it probably doesn't matter very much one way or the other.

Who has the chips also may be a factor in deciding whether to add on, especially in small hometown cardroom events with only two or three tables of players. If you see that a weak player who has been on a rush holds a top chip position, it probably is wise to make the add-on to give yourself additional ammunition to take advantage of his weak play. But if a very strong player holds top spot and you have a mid-sized stack, it probably won't increase your chances of a win enough to warrant adding on.

Don't make the mistake of adding on unnecessarily. Some players add on for "insurance purposes," but I suspect that fear also plays a part in their decision. The fear of losing the lead is a mental shadow that lurks in the dark corners of a leader's mind. Possibly the worst feeling I've had in a tournament is going into the final table as leader of the pack and finishing fourth with a three-spot payout. The fear of losing the lead, added to a dearth of good starting hands, led me to play too tight, not taking advantage of my table image or the few strong hands that I was dealt.

TIP 2: DESIGN YOUR GAME PLAN BEFORE YOU SIT DOWN

When you enter a tournament, you should always have your basic strategy in mind before making your buy-in. If you intend to rebuy, decide how many rebuys you're willing and can afford to make.

Decide in advance how you're going to play during each segment of the tournament. Tournaments have early rounds, middle rounds, late rounds, and final-table rounds. Experienced players design a game plan for each segment. You plan your play and then play your plan for as long as it is working for you. An example of a plan might be "I will play aggressively early, but use survival tactics in the late rounds. If I have a big stack, I will attack short stacks, but if I have a short stack, I will lay back. I will avoid big confrontations late in the tournament."

Billy, a natural born aggressor, always plays a strategy that is designed to win, even if he has to forfeit a place. Therefore, he goes against survival strategy in the late stages and attacks big stacks as well as short stacks. He is willing to lose it all to win it all, because (in his words), "There's such a big difference between first and fourth places, I have to push it all the way to make up for the times I haven't cashed."

On the other hand, Big Al decides in advance that he will make only one buy-in, no matter what, and will only add on if he's short-stacked and feels lucky. "If I get lucky just before the add-on but I'm still low on chips, I'll go for it," he says. "But if I'm not catching cards, I won't put one more cent into it." He bows out in favor of a ring game and waits until the next tournament for Lady Luck to smile on him.

TIP 3: PLAY AGGRESSIVE POKER EARLY IN A REBUY EVENT

The advantage of playing aggressively early in a tournament is that you can build a big stack to take into the later stages for intimidation and for driving out the short stacks. The disadvantage is that you stand to lose it all and will be forced to rebuy several times. If the reward appears to be worth the risk, take it. But if the play-fast strategy isn't working for you, ease off.

Don't mix up playing "fast" with playing loose. When you play loose, you play too many hands and pursue too many draws. When you play fast, you push your good draws to their fullest advantage. You raise and reraise to build a pot that will give you maximum value. You want to win as many chips right now as you possibly can. You can play faster during the rebuy period than you can after it is over. Your goal is to build a big stack for the later stages when you may need to play more conservatively and use survival tactics.

Some players are actually looking for a chance to throw their hands away to alleviate the stress of taking a big draw that may decimate their stacks. Help them out of their timid stance with boldness in the very early stages, especially if making rebuys is part of your tournament strategy.

One added note: In Omaha high-low rebuy tournaments, the tendency of many players is to play very tight. They wait for optimal starting hands in order to increase their chances of surviving to the last table. Often, they are the rocks who practice endless patience in their ring game strategy. This strategy is a viable option in Omaha high-low tournaments, particularly freeze-outs, though it is not highly recommended by most experts.

TIP 4: PRESERVE AND BUILD YOUR STACK AFTER THE REBUY PERIOD

With a short or medium stack, your goal in the later stages of the tournament is to survive the cut and come in for the money. Playing smart poker is especially important late in the tournament. You won't be taking high-risk draws, you won't push the edges, not will you raise for maximum value on hands that could be beaten on the river, unless you are in premium chip position against short stacks.

Preserving your good chip position is paramount. Several strategies will help you do that. One of them is not to get into a major confrontation with another big stack, even if you have an equal stack. You would rather get the small stacks out of action than risk your standing by going up against someone who is as strong or stronger than you are. Therefore, play more aggressively against short stacks and play tighter against big stacks.

No one likes to admit tournament errors, but I'll do it to demonstrate some not-so-smart late play. Early in my tournament career, I was playing at the Plaza in Downtown Las Vegas in a $40 rebuy tournament. I was in second chip position at the final table when the limits had risen to $1,000/$2,000. The big blind was all in, I was sitting immediately to his left, and I called with A-A-9-8 double suited. My goal was to take him out in a heads-up showdown. Thinking that everyone else at the table would realize my intentions and fold their hands, I was amazed when Goldie called with her tall stack.

When the flop came 9-5-4 with two of my suit, I bet and she called. On the turn came a 6. Believing that no sane person would enter a late pot with 8-7 in her hand, and having the nut-flush and inside-straight draws, I bet. Goldie raised. To call her raise, I had to go all in. Mistakenly, I did. A river ace gave me trips but Goldie turned over her 2-3-4-5 offsuit, the double nuts.

FLOP   **TURN**   **RIVER**

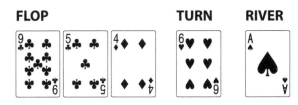

SHANE

GOLDIE

I had committed the ultimate tournament mistake in pitting myself against a player who had better position, a big stack, and (unfortunately) cards that fit the flop. I soothed my pain with a roll of nickels and a vengeful attack on a video poker machine.

TIP 5: ALWAYS BE AWARE OF YOUR STACK STATUS

Always be aware of your stack's status in relation to your opponents, and your seat position at the table. For example, if you are in very low stack status but in the big or small blind with the button coming up in one or two hands, be inclined to throw away your hand, even if it looks strong. Save your chips and wait for the button when you will have multiple opportunities to be dealt an optimal hand.

Suppose you are in the big blind and have enough money left for the small blind and perhaps two extra bets. The player on your left is very short on chips with only enough to meet the big and small blinds. Do not call a raise. Allow your short-stacked opponent the chance to go all in on the next two rounds.

If you are in strong chip status and good position with a reasonable hand, attack the weak blinds with a raise. If they fold, you own their chips. If they call, you have the positional advantage to raise them all-in and possibly eliminate them from the tournament with a favorable flop.

But if you are in good chip status and so is the player to your left, allow him to attack the blinds (provided you know that he is a strong tournament strategist), thus preserving your chips. The tall stacks usually try to get the blinds out of the game, if either or both blinds are in weak chip status.

Tournament leaders try to eliminate the weak stacks as soon as they can to reduce the competition and to further enhance their chances of winning. I recall a tournament in which one of the sophisticated players complained because Ben, one of the meek strong stacks, did not take out a short stack when he had the chance. He was right. That short stack rejuvenated himself and went on to take third place.

TIP 6: CALL MORE IN THE LATE LEAD

When you find yourself in strong chip position late in a tournament, you may be wise to call more often, especially against the short stacks. This is because you have less to lose than they do, and more to gain if they don't hit the flop. Even if you think you are the underdog, it is often correct to call.

Sometimes, a small stack can rebuild itself by just copping the antes or blinds, which may help him considerably. The small bet you must call will not especially hurt you, and it could help you a lot if the lower stack misses and is eliminated from competition.

TIP 7: YOU DON'T NEED AS STRONG A HAND IN SHORTHANDED PLAY

When it gets close to the end of a tournament with only two tables left in action, both tables will become increasingly shorthanded until the two are combined. As the number of players at your table decreases, you can decrease your starting hand requirements. This is true because you usually do not need as much strength to win a pot against only five opponents as you do against eight other players.

In Omaha high-low, then, you don't necessarily need to make the nut high or the nut low in order to win your share of the pot. The second-nut low or the third-nut high often are good enough. Whereas you may not have entered pots with a hand such as A♠ 4♦ 8♠ 9♣ in the early stages when you were playing nine-handed, this type of hand looks pretty good when you're playing five-handed, especially since you have a suited ace. High hands with danglers begin to look better against fewer opponents, so you might come in with a hand such as K-K-J-7, especially at a passive table in late position.

TIP 8: PLAY MORE HIGH HANDS IN THE LATE STAGES

Survival is a major consideration late in a tourney. You want hands that can win on the flop rather than ones that require a draw. As players are eliminated and there are fewer people in the pots, high hands gain value and low hands lose value because they usually require a draw and do best in multiway pots.

What you are looking for is a hand that can win the whole enchilada on the flop. Of course, if your low hand is A-2-3-K double suited, or any four-wheeler with a suited ace, then you are correct to enter the fray. With a hand that strong, you have the chance to win it all with a wheel, a flush, or even top two pair.

Final-stage pots are often played shorthanded. With only three players in a pot, your low draw usually has insufficient strength to make it worth the risk of playing. Even if you win the low half, the win probably will be too small to justify risking a lot to win very little. But if you hold a high hand with three people in the competition, you are often able to win the pot immediately if the flop comes with two high cards. In that case, the lows cannot afford to draw against you if only one low card comes on the flop.

TIP 9: BEWARE THE MANIACS

Maniacs are tournament maulers who assault their victims with a battery of preflop shenanigans and a barrage of reckless raises on post-flop drawing hands. All low-limit tournaments are heavily sprinkled with maniacs until the very late stages when most of them have been eliminated by the patient play of the rocks and the superior play of solid competitors who know how to avoid maniacs in the early stages and outplay them in the late stages.

If a maniac is sitting to your left, come in with your best hands only, ones with which you can call a raise. If a maniac raises in front of you, reraise if you have a superior hand. Otherwise, fold. Above all, don't get sucked into the undercurrent of wild betting created by these chip hogs who usually claim to be trying to build their stacks early with their loose play and multiple bets.

In tournaments, also be cautious about calling end bets that are made by weak players when a card comes that reduces your hand to second-best. In their ignorance, these weaklings often will chase with inferior hands that sometimes arrive at the river. The difference between the weak player and the maniac is that the weakling often doesn't understand what he's doing, but the maniac's actions are premeditated. Either one can torpedo your ship.

TIP 10: KEEP YOUR COOL WHEN THE STAKES GET HOT

You've watched enough poker tournaments on television to see how the crybabies act when an inferior hand outdraws them on the river. "How could you have played that hand?!" is a favorite line of the moaners and groaners who have no shame in expressing their childish emotions on national broadcasts.

You especially cannot allow your emotions to overwhelm you at the final table. That's where the money is, where the trophy is, where the braggin' rights are. You must keep your cool when the action gets hot. Don't blow it, stow it!

How? Back to the affirmations: "Play right. Wait, watch, win." You know the drill.

Omaha high can be brutal! It's a cold, cruel world and it's a cold, cruel game ... but it's not as cold and cruel as Omaha split, which is even more aggravating!

— *Tom McEvoy*

Remember that Omaha high-low is a two-tiered game. You play big hands or you play little hands. You do not play middle hands. You play Omaha high-low as though you were playing with a stripped deck, as though the sevens, eights and nines weren't in the deck. You say to yourself, "I can't win playing sevens, eights and nines in this game."

— *T. J. Cloutier*

Winston Churchill once described Russia as "a riddle wrapped in a mystery inside an enigma." I feel the same way about Omaha. At first brush, it seems such a simple game. Two cards from your hand, three from the board; no more, no less, no problem. Yeah, right, Omaha is the unfolding flower. The more you know about the game, the more you realize just how little you know.

— *John Vorhaus*

Chapter 11

Eight Costly Omaha Errors

Errors are warts on your poker skin, ugly things that everybody occasionally gets but nobody ever wants. Just as warts can be removed with medical treatment, you can cure your bad habits with Double-D medication: Desire and discipline. With a strong *desire* to become a winner and the personal *discipline* to change your habits, you are already on the road to recovery.

Poker players get paid when they make the right decisions, and are punished when they make the wrong ones. Mistakes mutilate money, minimize morale, and can put you on tilt, the worst of all poker warts. Here are eight costly errors Omaha high-low players make, plus some prescriptions to help you correct them.

1. PLAYING TOO MANY HANDS

Sitting around waiting for a good hand is boring work, and poker is about *playing*, right? Wrong! Poker is like fishing. Fishermen bait their hooks, throw their lines into the water ... and wait. When the fish finally bites, they must act quickly and alertly to reel it in. They bait. They wait. They react alertly. And then the cycle repeats itself.

You cannot drag any chips into your stack until you have some bait to reel them in with; that is, you need to play good starting hands. If you're not willing to wait for good cards, it is almost impossible to reel in a win at low-limit Omaha high-low.

This game can tempt you to play too many hands, especially when you are losing, which is the worst of all times to play more than you should. When you're losing, tighten up, don't loosen up. You need to get optimal value from the chips you have left. You may find that using the following affirmations will help you from allowing boredom and your natural desire for action overcome your common sense, which is Wise Wanda-Wendall's domain.

a. I play tight and right.
b. More tosses equal fewer losses.
c. I play only premium starting hands, no matter what.
d. If I wait and watch, I will win.

Another thing that you can do to prevent yourself from playing too many hands is to write a list of your starting requirements on the back of a business card. Then place the card between your stack and you. Read it before every flop. Winning players are controlled players. Because winners have strict standards for starting hands, they don't play nearly as many pots as their losing opponents.

2. MAKING TOO MANY CALLS

Calling stations are wonderful opponents to have in any poker game because they simply cannot lay down a second-best hand. They've never seen an Omaha high-low hand they didn't like and they use "I just wanted to keep you honest" as a poor excuse for making a bad call. Even experienced players sometimes call too often, usually because they fall in love with a "beautiful" hand and then cannot release it. But your beauties must fit the flop or they quickly become beasts.

If you find yourself getting into the habit of making too many calls, head for the bathroom. Look in the mirror and give yourself a stern talking to. (In the event that you're not alone, I suggest doing this mentally rather than audibly!) Say something like "Shane, you're making too many calls. Why? Are you getting desperate to win a pot? Are you angry because Joe bluffed you out of that big one and you want him to know that he can't get away with that again? Or are you just getting lazy? Are you too tired to play any longer?"

Whatever your answer, tell yourself to stop calling so much. Remind your ego that you're too good a player to adopt the habits of your inferiors. Then go back to the table and take your own advice.

The next time you make a loose call that costs you some chips, place that number of chips in a separate stack called your **misstack**. Each time you enter a pot, think of yourself as a businessman going into a new venture. Think of each call as an investment, your stack as your return on investment, and your misstack as a business loss. What is your percentage of return on your investment? How does the height of your misstack compare with the height of your stack?

3. MISREADING YOUR HAND

Never do so many bet so much with so little as do novices in low-limit Omaha high-low games. One calls at the river with a counterfeited low hand not realizing the impact of his duplicated ace on the river. Another bets his "straight" using three cards from his hand. Still another bets his "full house" using only one of his hole cards.

If you have difficulty in reading either or both ends of Omaha high-low hands, don't play another session until you've dealt at least 100 practice rounds and have done the following:

a. Deal nine hands around the kitchen table. Pretend that you are each player in turn. Bet, call or raise according to the strength of each hand. Then flop the first three common cards.

b. Analyze each hand on the flop, the turn and the river by asking, "What is the best possible low hand this player can make? What is the best possible high hand that he can make?" Bet, call, raise or fold for each hand.

c. Keep a record of the kinds of hands that win. Analyze your records and you will discover the level of strength that it usually takes to win most pots.

4. NOT READING YOUR OPPONENTS

At a motivational seminar I recently attended, the speaker advised us to "Enter the day slowly." He arises two hours before his workday begins, reads something inspirational, runs for 30 minutes, and then enters his day in the work place.

Enter your Omaha high-low game slowly. Observe the players in the ring for a while before you play a hand. Watch for their loose-tight index, their tells, their betting habits. What seems to be their favorite betting round? When are they most likely to raise? What kinds of hands do they usually play? Do they ever slowplay? Are they calling stations? Who appears to be on tilt? Who looks tired? Who is the rock? Who is the expert?

All superior poker players have a sixth sense about people. Develop it for yourself by watching others, especially when you are not in a hand. The earlier you can put a make on them, the better you can play against them. If you cannot read your opponents, you are like a blind man at a traffic signal, not knowing when to stop or go. Think of yourself as "working" poker rather than "playing" poker.

"If a wing fell off a gnat at the end of the table, I'd see it," T.J. Cloutier said in "Getting to Know Your Opponents," which is important enough to this world-class player to be Chapter One in his book, *Championship No-Limit & Pot-Limit Hold'em*.

5. TAKING A BIG LOSS AT ONE SITTING

Leaving the table as a loser is the one thing that most poker players hate to do more than anything else. This is the main reason why so many of us sometimes play for too many hours at a session or why we play to the point where we are no longer competitive, incapacitated by fatigue or frustration.

Omaha high-low can have wide fluctuations in fortune for loose players who enter pots with marginal hands. It is not unusual to see such a player's stack yo-yo. An accomplished player and tournament winner once advised me, "The secret is to stay even." If you observe the stacks of skilled players, you will notice that they don't rise and fall nearly as dramatically as the stacks of less disciplined opponents and those on tilt. (Try this valuable exercise in observation.)

To prevent yourself from taking a huge loss at any one session, you can use a stop-loss figure. I realize that this advice is contrary to the most astute poker theorists, who disclaim it as a stock market philosophy rather than a sound poker strategy but here it is anyway. Try setting a monetary amount that you easily can replace from outside sources in the event that you lose. For example, you decide in advance that you will leave the game if you are anywhere close to losing $200. When you are approaching your maximum level of discomfort in the losing zone, remind yourself, "There's always another day to play, another game in which I can be a winner. I don't have to stay here getting my brains knocked out trying to get it all back tonight." Then leave.

When I interviewed tournament champion Steve Rydell (who has won numerous big events, including a World Series title) for *Card Player* magazine, he told me, "When I'm losing, I want to leave. I just figure it's not my night. Not only that, if you're losing, the people who are winning are playing a nice, competent game. When I'm winning, that's when I want to stay. I never could understand why most people want to leave when they're winning but not when they're losing."

6. PLAYING IN A BAD GAME

A bad Omaha high-low game is one that has no loose players, but instead is filled with rocks and experts. If you look around for the pigeon and find none, you're probably it. These low-action, tight games are not where you want to play, particularly if you are not as good as the rest of the people at the table. As the saying goes, "If you want to be the best poker player in town, find the game with the worst players."

Another type of bad game may be one that doesn't fit your playing style. For example, if you are passive by nature and find yourself in a "no fold'em" Omaha game with maniacs who raise to the max before every flop and cap each pot on the turn, you are a fish out of your waters. Find another ocean in which to swim before you drown.

7. PLAYING FOR TOO LONG

Tired players often are losers. Their mental guidance capacities deteriorate like ships lost in a dense fog. Fatigue leads to mistakes and every mistake in poker is spelled *m-o-n-e-y.*

When you find yourself losing your edge, when you've made two or three costly errors in a row, when fatigue's crazy glue has you pasted to your chair, break the bonds and leave. Don't play past your peak performance period.

If you find yourself playing marathon sessions—which, in my experience, are more common among players in small hometown cardrooms with few other recreational options— you can use an alarm watch to remind yourself to go home. Or visit the john one more time, saying to the worn-out visage that stares back at you from the mirror with haggard eyes, "There's always another game tomorrow. Right now, I need rest more than I need the thrill of victory. And for sure, I don't need the agony of defeat!"

In marathon sessions, the agony often follows the ecstasy.

8. PLAYING WITH A DISADVANTAGE

A disadvantage is anything that keeps you from playing your best game. It may be a cold, a headache, a broken pinkie finger or some other physical disability. Often, it is your emotional frame of mind. If you arrive at the game still brooding over the argument you had with your teenager, your concentration is likely to seesaw between the game and your home situation. Or maybe you've just come off a long losing streak and are playing scared money.

Just before I sat down in a $10/$20 game in Las Vegas years ago, I discovered that I had been bilked out of $300 by a con man. Angry at both my vulnerability and my financial loss (and the lousy so-and-so), I blew off $700. Later, too much later, I recalled the advice of Doyle Brunson: "When a man's got something heavy on his mind besides poker, he's got no business playing. Brother, you just can't make critical decisions when you're going through personal agony."

Certain types of players may also pose a distraction to you. Garrulous talking machines annoy me (please don't spread the word), a friend hates sitting next to someone with heavy duty body odor, and my brother doesn't like being next to a guy who keeps asking questions about the game. My late buddy Tex Sheahan told the story of a game in which one of the world's most beautiful women was sitting "at the curve of the table, which was appropriate for her." Apparently, she was sweet as sugar as she picked the pockets of most of the male players in the ring.

Also, the house rake occasionally is so high that the price of playing poker becomes an albatross. In my opinion, this sometimes occurs when cardrooms install bad-beat jackpots. The rake not only includes the customary percentage but an added deduction for the jackpot pool. Be careful about the number of hands you play in these games because each pot you enter takes an extra percentage from your chips, just as an inept dentist might extract a tooth here, a tooth there, until you are forced to buy false teeth from him.

If you find yourself playing at a disadvantage, head for home. If you don't, you will be handicapping yourself with burdens too heavy for any horse to win the race.

Chapter 12

Seven Quick Review Tips for Winners at Omaha High-Low

You've read the advice in this book carefully and hopefully, you're going to win a lot of money at Omaha high-low. Now it's time to enjoy yourself at the tables and use your newfound skills to be a consistent winner at the game. But before you run off and start your new winning ways, I've boiled down some of the advice into seven concise winning tips. Let's get to 'em!

Winning Tip #1: Play Hands in Which All Four Cards Work Together in Harmony

As a beginner, play hands that will "play themselves" after the flop. Look for low hands that have an ace with a deuce, preferably suited, and one other wheel card (which will give you the extra out that you often need). High hands should contain four cards in sequence with as few gaps as possible, or a high pair with two related cards. You may feel as though you're constrained by a straight jacket, because you'll have to wait out myriad deals before catching these premium cards. Use your hiatus from action to watch the other players, noting the types of hands that are winning the pots. You'll soon learn the starting-hand strength necessary to beat the game.

Winning Tip #2: Fit or Fold

Why do so many amateurs lose so much money at Omaha high-low? Because they chase pots with beautiful hands that don't match the beastly flop. When you enter a pot, ask yourself, "What is the perfect flop for this hand?" If it doesn't come, fold and save yourself loads of fool's gold.

Some low-limit and beginning players will chase a flop such as K-Q-3 with hands like A-2-4-8. If another low card comes on the turn, they are often ready to call multiple raises hoping for a low river card. With no other outs, such as the A-2 suited to two flush cards on the board, or A-2-4-10, which offers an extra inside straight draw for the above board, always fold when your hand does not fit the flop.

Winning Tip #3: Draw Only to the Nuts

Why do so many beginners lose so many pots with the second-nut low, the second-best full house, flush or straight?

Because they draw to them. Why? Because they hope no one else holds the nuts. Hope is a four-letter word in Omaha high-low. Many readers have told me that one of the most useful axioms in my book is, "If it's possible, it's probable." If it is possible for a better hand to be made, it is probable that someone will make it. Just be sure that "someone" is you by drawing to the nuts. For example, don't draw to a king-high flush when the ace is not on the board and there is a lot of betting. And of course, don't draw to the ignorant end of a straight, especially a low straight where you'll probably wind up splitting the pot. If you play premium hands and draw only to the nuts, you can usually win money at this game no matter what limits you play.

Winning Tip #4: Play Premium High Hands in Late Position or Unraised Pots

As a novice, try to play premium high hands in late position or in unraised pots only. Many experienced Omaha high-low players are looking for the best low hand, one which can win the whole enchilada with a wheel; whereas Texas hold'em players new to Omaha high-low are accustomed to seeking the best high hand, not realizing that high hands lose value in this game. Ray Zee states that "high hands do well in situations where one or no low cards come on the flop. When two or three low cards come, these hands tend to do very poorly."

Winning Tip #5: Seldom Raise Before the Flop

Always try to see the flop as cheaply as possible. Low hands such as A-3-7-9 and high hands like Q-Q-J-10 are not raising hands, although you will see players habitually raise with these types of hands in low-limit games. Another tip:

The more raising before the flop, the more likely it is that one or more opponents holds A-2 suited with a third low card. This means that if you do not have an A-2 with backup wheel card(s), you probably have little chance of making the best low. And if you do have an A-2, you probably are not alone.

Winning Tip #6: Middle Cards and Low Pairs are Losers

I cannot think of a poker game in which middle cards are winners. In Texas hold'em, they often make the low (losing) end of a straight; in seven-card stud, two middle pair always lose to a high pair-low pair combination. And in Omaha high-low, hands such as 8-7-6-5 or 9-7-7-5 are spelled d-o-g. You're barking up the wrong tree with them.

Winning Tip #7: Omaha High-Low is a River Game

Omaha high-low is a drawing contest. You want a flop that immediately gives you either the best possible uncounterfeitable hand or a draw to that hand. In no other poker game do I hear more complaints that "they drew out on me at the river" than in Omaha high-low. Maybe that's why my uncle thinks this is a game enjoyed primarily by masochists.

Although many low-limit players try, it is nearly impossible to raise an opponent out of a pot if he believes that he can win it with a favorable river card. Players with the patience to wait for a premium starting hand can often outrun master strategists who use raising and bluffing ploys to try to force out strong drawing hands.

Omaha high-low offers you a great opportunity to win money if you play tight, study, and use some of these winning tips. See you at the tables!

Recommended Reading & Software

Championship Omaha (Omaha High-Low, Omaha High and Pot-Limit Omaha) by Cloutier and McEvoy could become your bible on how to win at Omaha high-low. Yes, it's that good! Of course, you won't find many high Omaha or pot-limit Omaha cash games these days because they're played primarily in tournament format. But don't let that deter you from reading this book—its emphasis is on Omaha high-low, with plenty of demonstration hands and tournament tips designed to turn you into a winning player. Another book in the "Championship Series" published by Cardoza Publishing.

Omaha High-Low (Winning Strategies for all 5,278 Omaha High-Low Hands) by Bill Boston is a must-have for serious players. No matter how low or how high the stakes you play, the odds for particular types of poker hands remain the same. Boston not only gives you the odds of winning the high, the low, or scooping the pot with every conceivable Omaha high-low hand, he tells you how to win more often by using the odds to your advantage. I was fortunate in working with Boston on a few of his strategy tips, and can vouch for the precision and strength of his recommended plays. A Cardoza Publishing publication.

Tournament Tips from the Poker Pros (How to Win Low-Limit Poker Tournaments) by Shane Smith. I first wrote this book in 1992 and updated it for today's structures and poker environment in 2008. Its value for beginning tournament players is in its simple explanation of elementary tournament principles. I clearly explain the fundamental concepts of tournament poker that so many pro players have buried in the back of their minds and take for granted that everybody knows. In the early days of poker, I self-published this book but later turned it over to the gaming world's largest publisher of poker books, Cardoza Publishing.

High-Low-Split Poker (Seven-Card Stud and Omaha 8-or-better) by Ray Zee describes two distinct versions of Omaha high-low: high limit and low limit. Malmuth believes that this is the only game in which there is such a vast difference between high and low-limit games. This excellent text is especially useful if you enjoy playing both versions of high-low split poker.

Omaha Hold'em Poker by Bob Ciaffone. One of the best books in print on high Omaha, although it primarily addresses pot-limit play. The "millennium" edition includes an excellent chapter on Omaha high-low from this noted poker player and columnist.

Cappelletti On Omaha by Michael A. Cappelletti. A good book on high Omaha, with a point count system to evaluate hands. Includes one chapter on Omaha high-low.

Caro On Gambling by Mike Caro. His journalistic style makes anything Caro writes both entertaining and instructional. "Eleven Ways to Lose Money Fast" is one of his provocative chapter titles. Caro's forte is psychology, so don't miss Chapter 3, "In Search of the Right Winning Attitude."

Turbo Omaha High-Low Split is a computer software program from Wilson Software. You can practice your ring game by choosing from several point-count options. Highly recommended by Mike Caro, this sophisticated software package allows you to evaluate your expertise and tutors you in optimal strategy.

Glossary

Chasing. The habit of attempting to draw out with inferior cards, an activity often engaged in by perpetual losers.

Counterfeited. One or more of your straight cards appears on the board, demoting the value of your hand. For example, you hold A-2-5-6 and the board shows 2-4-9, counterfeiting your deuce.

Draw Out. Make the best hand on the river, often incurring the wrath of other players in the hand.

Drawing Dead. Drawing for a card when you have no outs.

Fifth Street. The last common card turned over by the dealer in Omaha games. The river card.

Flop. The first three common cards the dealer spreads open on the table, generating pain or pleasure.

Fit the Flop. Every Omaha high-low player's dream: your hand dovetails with the flop cards.

Fourth Street. The fourth common card turned over by the dealer. The turn card.

Hogger. A hand that wins the entire pot, causing the winner to voice snorts, grunts and other melodious sounds.

Live Player. A loose player, often one who is new to the game and gets hooked into the action. A careless caller who is frequently outplayed by experts.

The Nuts. The best high or low hand; also, occasionally used to describe Omaha high-low players.

Nut High. The best possible high hand given the cards in play.

Nut Low. The lowest of the possible lows given the cards in play. Usually wins one-half the pot, sometimes one-fourth of it, but can win the whole thing to become a hogger.

Nut-Nut. A duo-syllabic pronouncement which stuttering braggadocios exclaim when they possess both the nut high and the nut low hands on the river.

Omaha High-low. A form of hold'em poker in which the pot is split between the best high and the best low (8-or-better) hands.

Outs. Cards yet to come which will improve your hand.

River. The fifth card of the flop. Destiny. A place where one makes or loses his fortune. The moment of truth in Omaha high-low.

Rivered. An event in which someone else makes a better hand than the hand you held on fourth street. Experiencing a sinking feeling.

Scoop. See "hogger." A scooper is a hand that wins it all.

Stack. The quantity of chips you have in front of you, the height of which may fluctuate dramatically in an Omaha high-low game if your play is too loose.

Turn. The fourth card of the flop, often bought at a dear price by players hoping to fill a set or make the nut low.

Uncounterfeitable. You hold cards that are either the nut low or the nut high and which cannot be beaten by any other card that may come on the turn or river.

Do what you can, with what you have, from where you are.

— *Teddy Roosevelt*

After he had finished a concert and gone backstage, violin virtuoso Fritz Kreisler heard someone say, "I'd give my life to play as you do!" He turned to look at the woman and replied, "Madam, I did."

No game is more exciting than tournament poker! After a couple of shots at it, regular play seems strictly vanilla.

— *Tex Sheahan*

GREAT CARDOZA POKER BOOKS
ADD THESE TO YOUR LIBRARY - ORDER NOW!

CRASH COURSE IN BEATING TEXAS HOLD'EM *by Avery Cardoza*. Perfect for beginning and somewhat experienced players who want to jump right in on the action and play cash games, local tournaments, online poker, and the big televised tournaments where millions of dollars can be made. Both limit and no-limit hold'em games are covered along with the essential strategies needed to play profitably on the preflop, flop, turn, and river. The good news is that you don't need to memorize hands or be burdened by math to be a winner—just play by the no-nonsense basic principles outlined here. 208 pages, $14.95

INTERNET HOLD'EM POKER *by Avery Cardoza*. Learn how to get started in the exciting world of online poker. The book concentrates on Internet no-limit hold'em, but also covers limit and pot-limit hold'em, five- and seven-card stud, and Omaha. You'll learn everything from how to play and bet safely online to playing multiple tables, using early action buttons, and finding easy opponents. Cardoza gives you the largest collection of online-specific strategies in print—more than 6,500 words dedicated to 25 unique strategies! You'll also learn how to get sign-up bonuses worth hundreds of dollars! 176 pages, $9.95

HOW TO PLAY WINNING POKER *by Avery Cardoza*. New and completely updated, this classic has sold more than 250,000 copies. Includes major new coverage on playing and winning tournaments, online poker, limit and no-limit hold'em, Omaha games, seven-card stud, and draw poker (including triple draw). Includes 21 essential winning concepts of poker, 15 concepts of bluffing, how to use psychology and body language to get an extra edge, plus information on playing online poker. 256 pages, $14.95.

POKER TALK: Learn How to Talk Poker Like a Pro *by Avery Cardoza*. This fascinating and fabulous collection of colorful poker words, phrases, and poker-speak features more than 2,000 definitions. No longer is it enough to know how to walk the walk in poker, you need to know how to talk the talk! Learn what it means to go all in on a rainbow flop with pocket rockets and get it cracked by cowboys, put a bad beat on a calling station, and go over the top of a producer fishing with a gutshot to win a big dime. You'll soon have those railbirds wondering what *you* are talking about. 304 pages, $9.95.

OMAHA HIGH-LOW: Play to Win with the Odds *by Bill Boston*. Selecting the right hands to play is the most important decision to make in Omaha. This is the *only* book that shows you the chances that every one of the 5,278 Omaha high-low hands has of winning the high end of the pot, the low end of it, and how often it is expected to scoop all the chips. You get all the vital tools needed to make critical preflop decisions based on the results of more than 500 million computerized hand simulations. You'll learn the 100 most profitable starting cards, trap hands to avoid, 49 worst hands, 30 ace-less hands you can play for profit, and the three bandit cards you must know to avoid losing hands. 248 pages, $19.95.

TOURNAMENT TIPS FROM THE POKER PROS *by Shane Smith*. Essential advice from poker theorists, authors, and tournament winners on the best strategies for winning the big prizes at low-limit rebuy tournaments. Learn the best strategies for each of the four stages of play—opening, middle, late and final—how to avoid 26 potential traps, advice on rebuys, aggressive play, clock-watching, inside moves, top 20 tips for winning tournaments, and more. Advice from McEvoy, Caro, Malmuth, Ciaffone, others. 160 pages, $14.95.

NO-LIMIT TEXAS HOLD 'EM: The New Player's Guide to Winning Poker's Biggest Game *by Brad Daugherty & Tom McEvoy*. For experienced limit players who want to play no-limit or rookies who has never played before, two world champions show readers how to evaluate the strength of a hand, determine the amount to bet, understand opponents' play, plus how to bluff and when to do it. Seventy-four game scenarios, unique betting charts for tournament play, and sections on essential principles and strategies show you how to get to the winners circle. Special section on beating online tournaments. 288 pages, $24.95.

GREAT CARDOZA POKER BOOKS
ADD THESE TO YOUR LIBRARY - ORDER NOW!

HOLD'EM WISDOM FOR ALL PLAYERS *By Daniel Negreanu.* Superstar poker player Daniel Negreanu provides 50 easy-to-read and right-to-the-point hold'em strategy nuggets that will immediately make you a better player at cash games and tournaments. His wit and wisdom makes for great reading; even better, it makes for killer winning advice. Conversational, straightforward, and educational, this book covers topics as diverse as the top 10 rookie mistakes to bullying bullies and exploiting your table image. 176 pages, $14.95.

MILLION DOLLAR HOLD'EM: Winning Big in Limit Cash Games by *Johnny Chan and Mark Karowe.* Learn how to win money consistently at limit hold'em, poker's most popular cash game, from one of poker's living legends. You'll get a rare opportunity to get into the mind of the man who has won ten World Series of Poker titles—tied for the most ever with Doyle Brunson—as Johnny picks out illustrative hands and shows how he thinks his way through the betting and the bluffing. No book so thoroughly details the thought process of how a hand is played, the alternative ways it could have been played, and the best way to win session after session. *Essential* reading for cash players. 400 pages, $29.95.

THE POKER TOURNAMENT FORMULA by *Arnold Snyder.* Start making money now in fast no-limit hold'em tournaments with these radical and never-before-published concepts and secrets for beating tournaments. You'll learn why cards don't matter as much as the dynamics of a tournament—your position, the size of your chip stack, who your opponents are, and above all, the structure. Poker tournaments offer one of the richest opportunities to come along in decades. Every so often, a book comes along that changes the way players attack a game and provides them with a big advantage over opponents. Gambling legend Arnold Snyder has written such a book. 368 pages, $19.95.

HOW TO BEAT SIT-AND-GO POKER TOURNAMENTS by *Neil Timothy.* There is a lot of dead money up for grabs in the lower limit sit-and-gos and Neil Timothy shows you how to go and get it. The author, a professional player, shows you how to reach the last six places of lower limit sit-and-go tournaments four out of five times and then how to get in the money 25-35 percent of the time using his powerful, proven strategies. This book can turn a losing sit-and-go player into a winner, and a winner into a bigger winner. Also effective for the early and middle stages of one-table satellites.184 pages, $14.95.

HOW TO BEAT LOW-LIMIT POKER by *Shane Smith and Tom McEvoy.* If you're a low-limit player frustrated by poor results or books written by high-stakes players for big buy-in games, this is exactly the book you need! You'll learn how to win big money at the little games—$1/$2, $2/$4, $4/$8, $5/$10—typically found in casinos, cardrooms and played in home poker games. After one reading, you'll lose less, win more and play with increased confidence. You'll learn the top 10 tips and winning strategies specifically designed for limit hold'em, no-limit hold'em, Omaha high-low and low-limit poker tournaments. Great practical advice for new players. 184 pages, $9.95..

I'M ALL IN: High Stakes, Big Business, and the Birth of the World Poker *Tour* by *Lyle Berman with Marvin Karlins.* Lyle Berman recounts how he revolutionized and revived the game of poker and transformed America's culture in the process. Get the inside story of the man who created the World Poker Tour, plus the exciting world of high-stakes gambling where a million dollars can be won or lost in a single game. Lyle reveals the 13 secrets of being a successful businessman, how poker players self-destruct, the 7 essential principles of winning at poker. Foreword by Donald Trump. Hardback, photos. 232 pages, $24.95.

7-CARD STUD: The Complete Course in Winning at Medium & Lower Limits by *Roy West.* Learn the latest strategies for winning at $1-$4 spread-limit up to $10/$20 fixed-limit games. Covers starting hands, 3rd-7th street strategy, overcards, selective aggressiveness, reading hands, pro secrets, psychology, and more in an informal 42 lesson format. Includes bonus chapter on 7-stud tournament strategy by Tom McEvoy. 224 pages, $19.95.

THE CHAMPIONSHIP SERIES
POWERFUL INFORMATION YOU **MUST** HAVE

CHAMPIONSHIP NO-LIMIT & POT-LIMIT HOLD'EM *by T. J. Cloutier & Tom McEvoy.* The bible for winning pot-limit and no-limit hold'em tournaments gives you all the answers to your most important questions: How do you get inside your opponents' heads and learn how to beat them at their own game? How can you tell how much to bet, raise, and reraise in no-limit hold'em? When can you bluff? How do you set up your opponents in pot-limit hold'em so that you can win a monster pot? What are the best strategies for winning no-limit and pot-limit tournaments, satellites, and supersatellites? Rock-solid and inspired advice you can bank on from two of the most recognizable figures in poker. 304 pages, $29.95.

CHAMPIONSHIP HOLD'EM *by T. J. Cloutier & Tom McEvoy.* Hard-hitting hold'em the way it's played *today* in both limit cash games and tournaments. Get killer advice on how to win more money in rammin'-jammin' games, kill-pot, jackpot, shorthanded, and full table cash games. You'll learn the thinking process for preflop, flop, turn, and river play with specific suggestions for what to do when good or bad things happen. Includes play-by-play analyses, advice on how to maximize profits against rocks in tight games, weaklings in loose games, experts in solid games, plus tournament strategies for small buy-in, big buy-in, rebuy, add-on, satellite and big-field major tournaments. Wow! 392 pages, $29.95.

CHAMPIONSHIP OMAHA (Omaha High-Low, Pot-limit Omaha, Limit High Omaha) *by Tom McEvoy & T.J. Cloutier.* Clearly-written strategies and powerful advice from Cloutier and McEvoy who have won four World Series of Poker Omaha titles. You'll learn how to beat low-limit and high-stakes games, play against loose and tight opponents, and the differing strategies for rebuy and freezeout tournaments. Learn the best starting hands, when slowplaying a big hand is dangerous, what danglers are (and why winners don't play them), why you sometimes fold the nuts on the flop and would be correct in doing so, and overall, how you can win a lot of money at Omaha! 296 pages, illustrations, $29.95.

CHAMPIONSHIP HOLD'EM TOURNAMENT HANDS *by T. J. Cloutier & Tom McEvoy.* An absolute must for hold'em tournament players, two legends show you how to become a winning tournament player at both limit and no-limit hold'em games. Get inside the authors' heads as they think their way through the correct strategy at 57 limit and no-limit starting hands. Cloutier & McEvoy show you how to use skill and intuition to play strategic hands for maximum profit in real tournament scenarios and how 45 key hands were played by champions in turnaround situations at the WSOP. Gain tremendous insights into how tournament poker is played at the highest levels. 368 pages, $29.95.

CHAMPIONSHIP HOLD'EM SATELLITE STRATEGY *by Brad Dougherty & Tom McEvoy.* Every year satellite players win their way into the $10,000 WSOP buy-in and emerge as millionaires or champions. You can too! Learn the specific, proven strategies for winning almost any satellite from two world champions. Covers the ten ways to win a seat at the WSOP, how to win limit hold'em and no-limit hold'em satellites, one-table satellites, online satellites, and the final table of super satellites. Includes a special chapter on no-limit hold'em satellites! 320 pages, $29.95.

HOW TO WIN THE CHAMPIONSHIP: Hold'em Strategies for the Final Table, *by T.J. Cloutier.* If you're hungry to win a championship, this is the book that will pave the way! T.J. Cloutier, the greatest tournament poker player ever—he has won 60 major tournament titles and appeared at 39 final tables at the WSOP, both more than any other player in the history of poker—shows how to get to the final table where the big money is made and then how to win it all. You'll learn how to build up enough chips to make it through the early and middle rounds and then how to employ T.J.'s own strategies to outmaneuver opponents at the final table and win championships. You'll learn how to adjust your play depending upon stack sizes, antes/blinds, table position, opponents styles, chip counts, and the specific strategies for six-handed, three handed, and heads-up play. 288 pages, $29.95.

POWERFUL WINNING POKER SIMULATIONS
A MUST FOR SERIOUS PLAYERS WITH A COMPUTER!
IBM compatible CD ROM Win 95, 98, 2000, NT, ME, XP

These incredible full color poker simulations are the best method to improve your game. Computer opponents play like real players. All games let you set the limits and rake and have fully programmable players, plus stat tracking, and Hand Analyzer for starting hands. MIke Caro, the world's foremost poker theoretician says, "Amazing... a steal for under $500... get it, it's great." Includes free phone support. "Smart Advisor" gives expert advice for every play!

1. TURBO TEXAS HOLD'EM FOR WINDOWS - $59.95. Choose which players, and how many (2-10) you want to play, create loose/tight games, and control check-raising, bluffing, position, sensitivity to pot odds, and more! Also, instant replay, pop-up odds, Professional Advisor keeps track of play statistics. Free bonus: Hold'em Hand Analyzer analyzes all 169 pocket hands in detail and their win rates under any conditions you set. Caro says this "hold'em software is the most powerful ever created." Great product!

2. TURBO SEVEN-CARD STUD FOR WINDOWS - $59.95. Create any conditions of play; choose number of players (2-8), bet amounts, fixed or spread limit, bring-in method, tight/loose conditions, position, reaction to board, number of dead cards, and stack deck to create special conditions. Features instant replay. Terrific stat reporting includes analysis of starting cards, 3-D bar charts, and graphs. Play interactively and run high speed simulation to test strategies. Hand Analyzer analyzes starting hands in detail. Wow!

3. TURBO OMAHA HIGH-LOW SPLIT FOR WINDOWS - $59.95. Specify any playing conditions; betting limits, number of raises, blind structures, button position, aggressiveness/passiveness of opponents, number of players (2-10), types of hands dealt, blinds, position, board reaction, and specify flop, turn, and river cards! Choose opponents and use provided point count or create your own. Statistical reporting, instant replay, pop-up odds high speed simulation to test strategies, amazing Hand Analyzer, and much more!

4. TURBO OMAHA HIGH FOR WINDOWS - $59.95. Same features as above, but tailored for Omaha High only. Caro says program is "an electrifying research tool...it can clearly be worth thousands of dollars to any serious player. A must for Omaha High players.

5. TURBO 7 STUD 8 OR BETTER - $59.95. Brand new with all the features you expect from the Wilson Turbo products: the latest artificial intelligence, instant advice and exact odds, play versus 2-7 opponents, enhanced data charts that can be exported or printed, the ability to fold out of turn and immediately go to the next hand, ability to peek at opponents hand, optional warning mode that warns you if a play disagrees with the advisor, and automatic mode that runs up to 50 tests unattended. Tough computer players vary their styles for a great game.

---

6. TOURNAMENT TEXAS HOLD'EM - $39.95

Set-up for tournament practice and play, this realistic simulation pits you against celebrity look-alikes. Tons of options let you control tournament size with 10 to 300 entrants, select limits, ante, rake, blind structures, freezeouts, number of rebuys and competition level of opponents. Pop-up status report shows how you're doing vs. the competition. Save tournaments in progress to play again later. Additional feature allows quick folds on finished hands.